BASKETBALLOGY

Supercool Facts You Never Knew

Written and Illustrated by

Kevin Sylvester

annick press
toronto + berkeley

© 2017 Kevin Sylvester (text and illustrations)
Edited by Linda Pruessen
Designed by Sheryl Shapiro

The charts and graphs in this book are meant for illustrative purposes only and do not necessarily reflect exact ratios or measurements.

We acknowledge the support of the Canada Council for the Arts and the Ontario Arts Council, and the participation of the Government of Canada/la participation du gouvernement du Canada for our publishing activities.

Funded by the Government of Canada

Financé par le gouvernement du Canada

ONTARIO ARTS COUNCIL
CONSEIL DES ARTS DE L'ONTARIO
an Ontario government agency
un organisme du gouvernement de l'Ontario

Cataloging in Publication

Sylvester, Kevin, author
      Basketballogy : supercool facts you never knew / Kevin Sylvester.

Includes index.
Issued also in electronic formats.
ISBN 978-1-55451-932-3 (hardcover).—ISBN 978-1-55451-931-6 (softcover)
ISBN 978-1-55451-934-7 (PDF).—ISBN 978-1-55451-933-0 (EPUB)

      1. Basketball—Miscellanea—Juvenile literature. I. Title.
GV885.1.S95 2017   j796.323   C2017-901401-3
                                                    C2017-901402-1

Published in the U.S.A. by Annick Press (U.S.) Ltd.
Distributed in Canada by University of Toronto Press.
Distributed in the U.S.A. by Publishers Group West.

Printed in China

www.annickpress.com
www.kevinsylvesterbooks.com

Also available in e-book format. Please visit www.annickpress.com/ebooks.html for more details.

To Noah, Sara, Zev, Judah, and Ellie—My Basketball Buds

—K.S.

CONTENTS

INTRODUCTION

You may have heard baseball and football referred to as "America's pastimes," but that title really belongs to basketball. Unlike a lot of other sports, which grew out of field games such as rugby or cricket, basketball is a wholly North American invention, created without any previous rules to build on.

In December 1891, teacher James Naismith looked out the window of his school, in Springfield, Massachusetts, and saw snow, snow, and more snow. Outdoor sports—the normal recreation for his students—were out.

But Naismith, a Canadian who knew how to deal with being cooped up inside during many a blizzard, had a sudden inspiration. He nailed some peach baskets to the walls of the gym, called the stir-crazy young men in, and tossed them an old soccer ball. The goal was simple, he said: throw the ball in the other team's basket.

There were only 13 rules, and he made them up. (Check out pages 82 and 83 for the list.) The boys loved it! And they spread the word quickly. The game exploded. Women's schools picked up the new sport just a few months later.

Then the game went global. Naismith published the rules in the newsletter for the YMCA (Young Men's Christian Association), which had communities across the world. Within a year, players were tossing balls into baskets in Canada and France. Soon after that, the game spread to Japan, China, India, and beyond.

The genius of basketball is its simplicity. But science, math, and creative thinking have taken the basic game and transformed the way players think about what they do.

Players have grown in size. So have salaries and attendance. The rules have been adapted over time to keep the game moving and the fans entertained. And a split second can mean the difference between getting a "swish" basket and getting your shot whacked back into your face.

Simple? No way. Cool? You bet. Read on and see just how amazing North America's true pastime really is.

PEACH BASKETS AND BLIZZARDS

James Naismith didn't know he was creating a global game when he called those stir-crazy boys into the gym in 1891. He just wanted to keep his students active.

Naismith nailed peach baskets into the balcony that ran around the top level of the gym. Those baskets were 10 feet (3.04 meters) from the floor, and that's remained the official height ever since.

The first game was, in Naismith's own words, a bit of a free-for-all.

"Before I could pull them apart, one boy was knocked out, several of them had black eyes, and one had a dislocated shoulder. It certainly was murder." —James Naismith

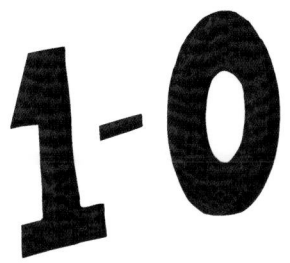

It was so difficult for the players to move that the winning team made only one basket, a 25-foot (7.62-meter) shot by a guy named William Chase. So Naismith drew up some rules to stop the roughhousing and get things moving. No more holding. No more tackling. Scoring increased. Injuries decreased. The game grew.

HURRY AND WAIT

Originally, when someone scored a basket, the game stopped—at least till the janitor could get a ladder to retrieve the ball. Naismith finally figured out if they cut the bottom out of the basket, the ball could go through, and the game could resume quickly. Eureka!

The first metal basket was manufactured in the late 1890s.

The backboard appeared in 1895 to stop spectators from reaching for the ball. They were originally made of wood; today, they are made of Plexiglas.

The netting was added to help officials see when a ball had actually gone through the hoop. That *swish* sound basketball players love to hear happens when a spinning ball is slowed down by the netting.

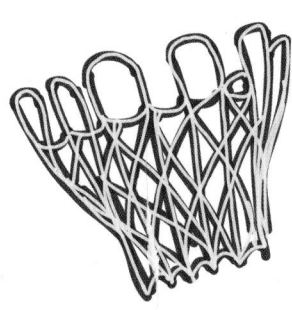

FOLLOW THE BOUNCING BALL

Naismith used an old soccer ball for the first game and for a few years after that, but once dribbling (bouncing the ball) became the norm, something bouncier was needed.

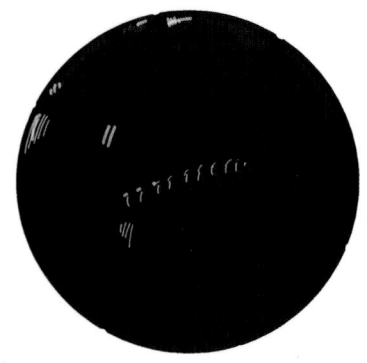

In 1894, Naismith and the Spalding company (who were also the first baseball manufacturer) designed a ball with a rubber bladder and a leather covering.

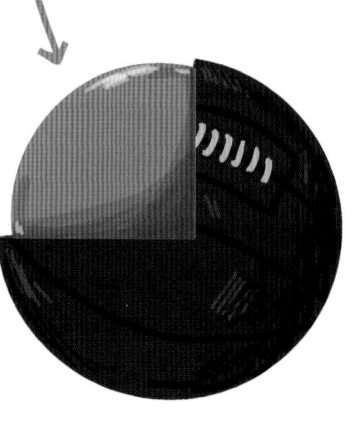

Ever wonder what that little hole is on a basketball? It's the inflation hole that lets you inflate the bladder inside the ball. But you need a special pin to do that.

In 1894, the laces originally ran along the outside seams to stitch the covering together.

The laces were removed in the 1930s.

The orange ball we know today was developed in the 1950s.

← 9.5 in (24.1 cm) diameter →

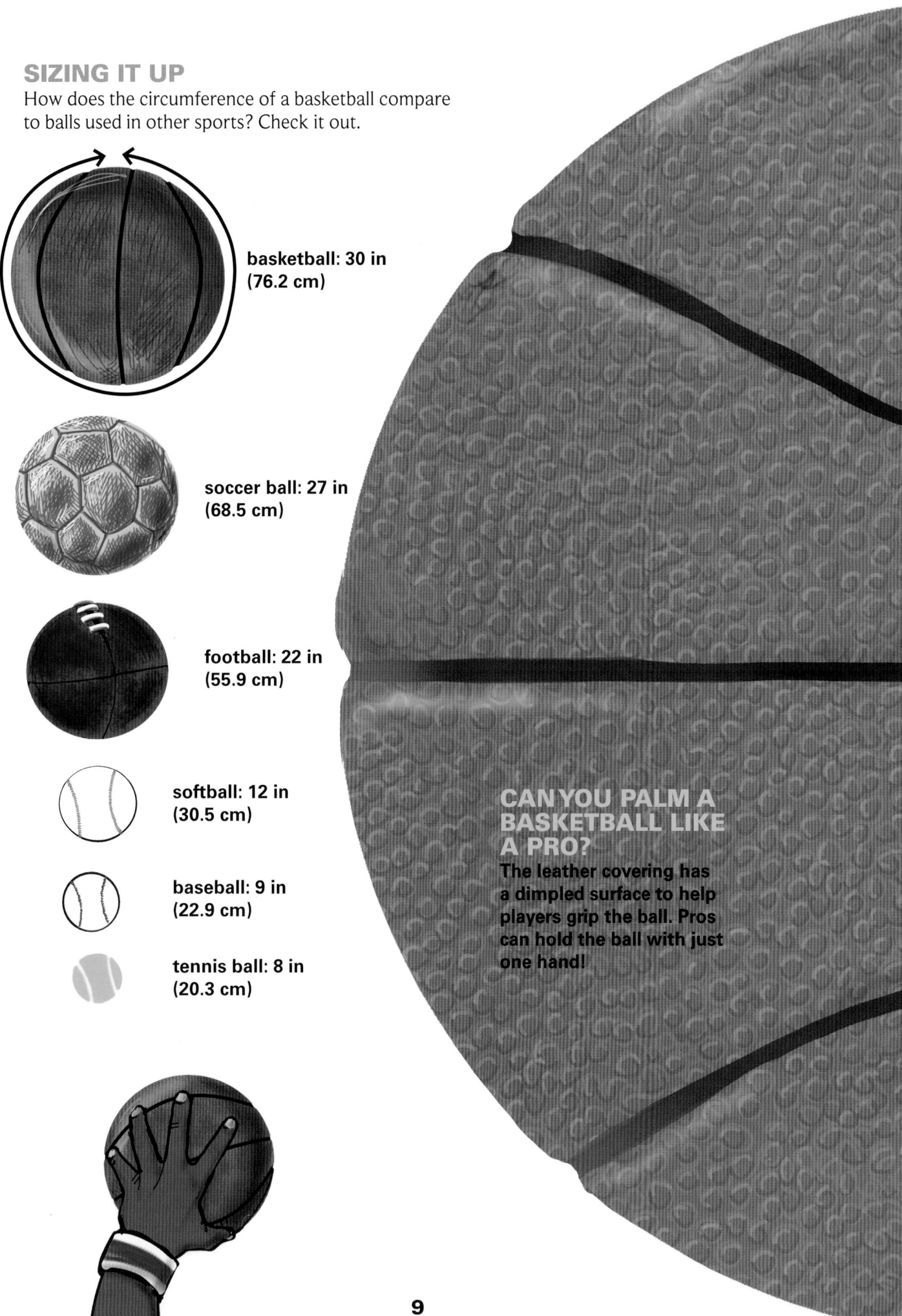

SIZING IT UP

How does the circumference of a basketball compare to balls used in other sports? Check it out.

basketball: 30 in (76.2 cm)

soccer ball: 27 in (68.5 cm)

football: 22 in (55.9 cm)

softball: 12 in (30.5 cm)

baseball: 9 in (22.9 cm)

tennis ball: 8 in (20.3 cm)

CAN YOU PALM A BASKETBALL LIKE A PRO?

The leather covering has a dimpled surface to help players grip the ball. Pros can hold the ball with just one hand!

WOOD YOU LIKE TO PLAY A GAME?

The first game was played on a floor designed for gymnastics and other exercises. It was only 54 by 35 feet (16.45 by 10.66 meters), roughly half the size of the average modern school gym. But, as the game grew, so did the court.

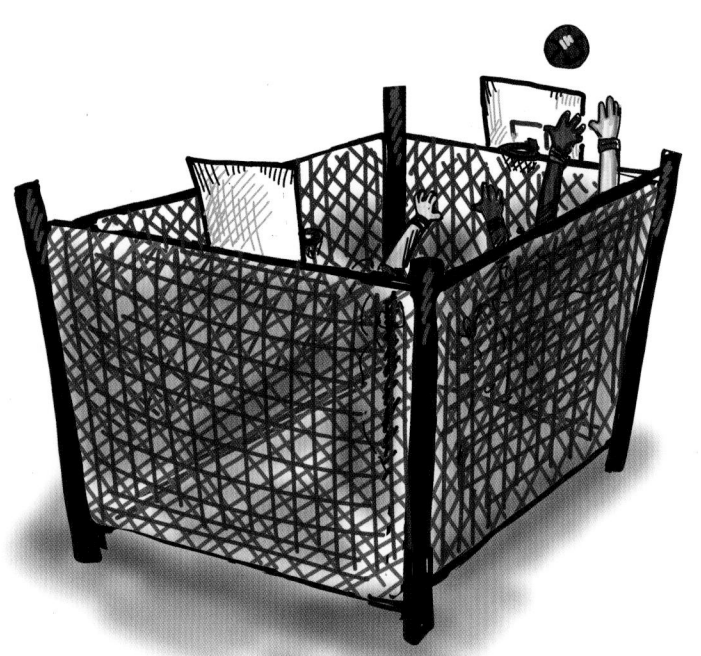

Basketball courts could be as small or as large as the arena allowed. Pro games were held in open ballrooms or indoor arenas. To limit the size of the court and to keep fans safe from flying basketballs—or bodies—teams set up wire barriers. An early version was made of chicken wire, which (not surprisingly) led to *many* cuts and scrapes. Later versions were made of rope or chains. The practice was scrapped in the 1920s, but basketball players have been called "cagers" ever since.

In 1924, as the pro game began to develop, teams got tired of shifting court sizes, chicken wire, and chains. It was time for standard court dimensions.

They set the court size as 60 to 95 feet (18.28 to 28.95 meters) long by 50 feet (15.24 meters) wide, depending on the space. They didn't have purpose-built basketball arenas then.

Modern pro courts: 94 by 50 feet (28.65 by 15.24 meters)

International courts (e.g., the ones at the Olympics): 92 by 49 feet (28.04 by 14.93 meters)

High school courts: 84 by 50 feet (25.60 by 15.24 meters)

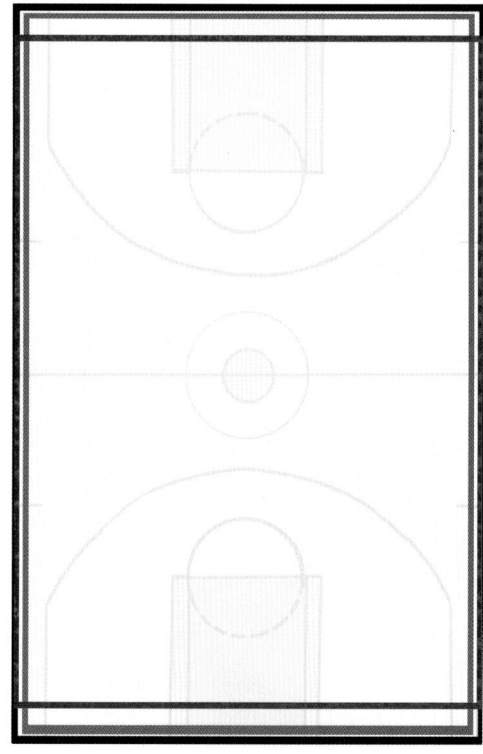

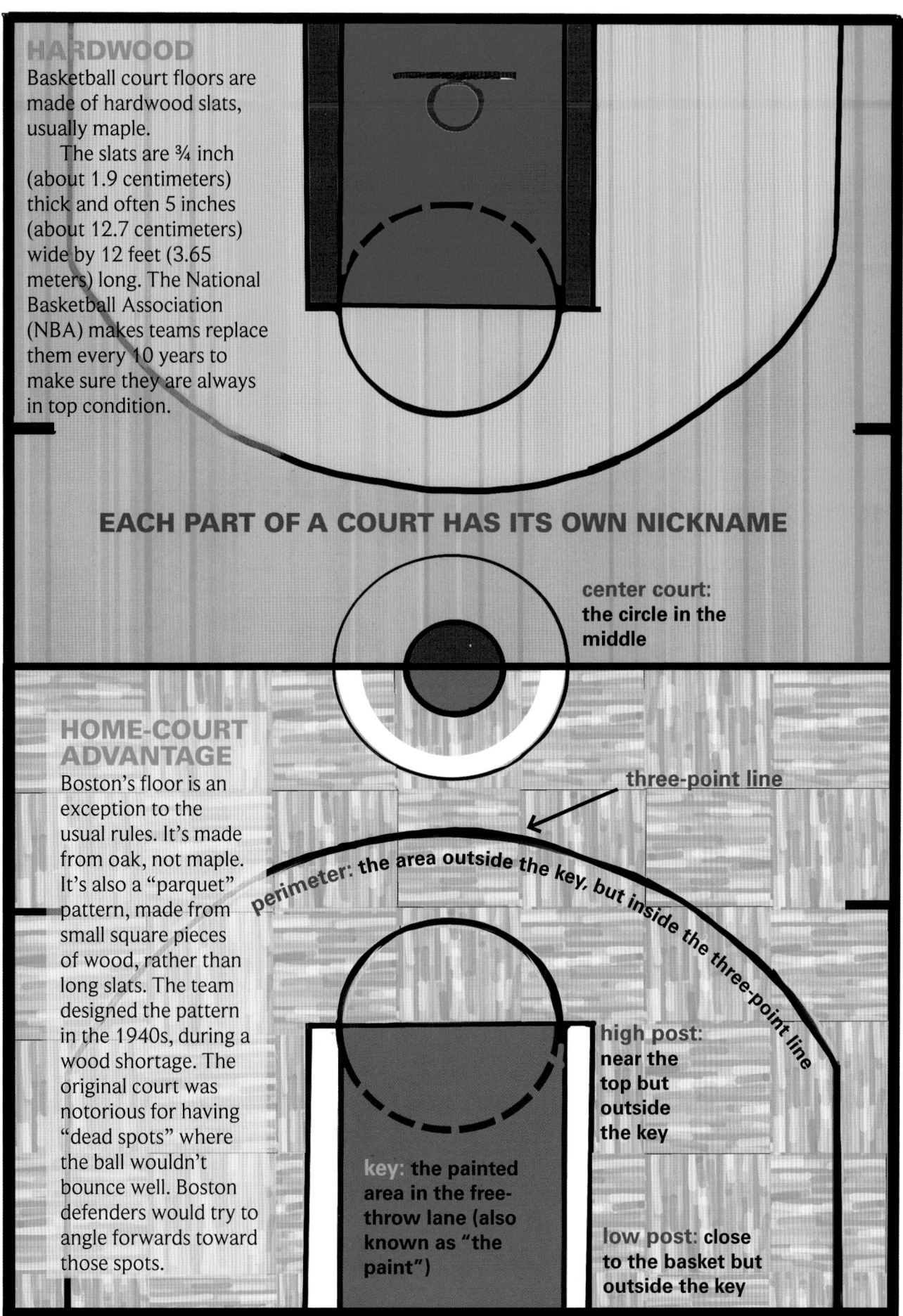

HARDWOOD

Basketball court floors are made of hardwood slats, usually maple.

The slats are ¾ inch (about 1.9 centimeters) thick and often 5 inches (about 12.7 centimeters) wide by 12 feet (3.65 meters) long. The National Basketball Association (NBA) makes teams replace them every 10 years to make sure they are always in top condition.

EACH PART OF A COURT HAS ITS OWN NICKNAME

center court: the circle in the middle

three-point line

HOME-COURT ADVANTAGE

Boston's floor is an exception to the usual rules. It's made from oak, not maple. It's also a "parquet" pattern, made from small square pieces of wood, rather than long slats. The team designed the pattern in the 1940s, during a wood shortage. The original court was notorious for having "dead spots" where the ball wouldn't bounce well. Boston defenders would try to angle forwards toward those spots.

perimeter: the area outside the key, but inside the three-point line

high post: near the top but outside the key

key: the painted area in the free-throw lane (also known as "the paint")

low post: close to the basket but outside the key

baselines: the lines at the ends of the court

DON'T QUIBBLE WITH THE DRIBBLE

Basketball has seen a lot of innovations over the years, most designed to speed up the game. Dribbling was the first big one—and today, you can't imagine the sport without it.

The first basketball rules indicated that players needed to throw, or "pass," the ball to get closer to the basket.

Naismith wanted the players to share. But it was way too easy to stand in front of somebody to stop them from throwing the ball. In the early days, opposing players would tackle or hold the player with the ball, preventing them from doing pretty much anything.

So, some ingenious players came up with a way to pass the ball to *themselves*—by bouncing it forward and then catching up. The dribble was born!

It wasn't *against* the rules. They weren't running with the ball, after all.

Naismith liked the idea. It kept the game moving and reduced the urge to tackle.

Yale University's men's team was the first to use dribbling in a game, in 1897. Early rules allowed only one bounce. But by 1909, players were allowed to dribble indefinitely, as long as they didn't pick up the ball and carry it (known as traveling), or "double-dribble" (stopping and starting again).

WOMEN'S RULES

Women have been playing basketball since the beginning, although with slightly different rules. Initially, there were nine players a side instead of five. And they had to stay inside set zones, to prevent contact. Dribbling was allowed, but it was limited. Even in the 1950s, women players were only allowed to dribble three times before they had to pass or shoot.

Look at old footage of basketball players and you'll see basic dribbling. But players have developed dozens of variations. Behind the back. Through the legs. Around another player. As long as you don't carry the ball or stop, you can be as creative as you want.

TICK-TOCK!

The introduction of the shot clock is arguably the *biggest* change to the speed of the game.

Teams *have* to attempt to shoot within 24 seconds of getting the ball. They don't have to make a basket, but the ball does need to at least touch the rim. This has led to an increase in scoring. Why?

Before the shot clock, players could hold on to the ball indefinitely to protect a lead. The only way to force a turnover was to foul a player on purpose and force them to shoot free throws. **BORING!***

In the 1953/54 season, the year before the shot clock was introduced, the average score was 79 points a game per team. The year after? A whopping 93 points per team. The average has hovered around 100 points per team ever since.

79 points per team

1953–1954

93 points per team

1954–1955

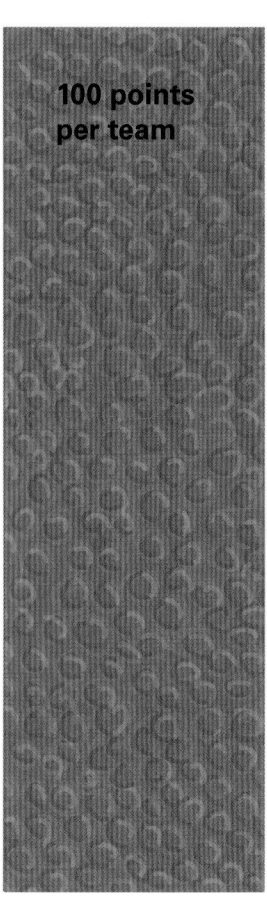

100 points per team

Today

*HOW BORING WAS IT?

On November 22, 1950, Fort Wayne beat Minneapolis 19–18. The two teams scored a grand total of *eight* baskets. The rest of the points came on foul shots.

In 1953, Boston and Syracuse battled it out in a play-off game that featured 106 fouls. Bob Cousy scored 30 points from the foul line.

In 1954, Syracuse beat New York 75–69 in another foul-filled play-off game. The teams combined for 75 free throws.

A "turnover" is when a team loses the ball to the other team without taking a shot. There are lots of ways to do this. They can make a bad pass. Go out of bounds. Double-dribble. Have the ball stolen from them. Good teams will turn the ball over about 12 times a game. Bad teams? Closer to 20.

TIMING IS EVERYTHING

Basketball games move really fast, and the ability to shoot quickly can be the difference between taking a shot or having the ball smashed back in your face.

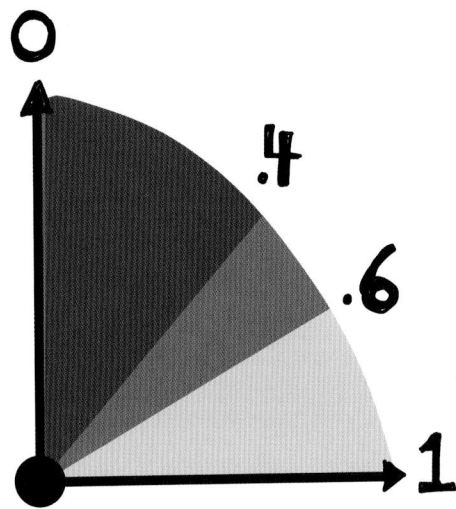

A basketball player has less than a second to get off the shot. In that time, they have to set, aim, and then shoot—all while a defender is trying to block the shot.

Steph Curry is probably the fastest shooter of all time. He's able to set and shoot in **0.4 seconds**—0.2 faster than the league average. And he's incredibly accurate. In 2015/16, he made 402 three-point shots. That smashed his *own* record of 286, set the season before.

ON THE REBOUND

Defenders try to rush the shooter, forcing them to hurry their shot and miss. If they miss, the ball is up for grabs. When a player grabs the ball after a missed shot, it's called a "rebound." If a player on the shooting team gets the ball, it's an offensive rebound, and the team gets **24 seconds** to shoot again. If the defensive team gets it, they get **24 seconds** to head back down the other way and shoot.

Big players often slam into one other fighting for the ball on a rebound. If they grab it at the same time, with no one getting clear possession, the officials call a "jump ball." Then the players have to leap up and grab the ball after an official tosses it in the air.

DON'T JUST STAND THERE!

Defenders can't just stand and wait for a miss. The foul-shot lane ("the paint") also doubles as the three-second defensive zone. Defensive players in this zone commit a foul if they stand there for longer than three seconds without defending against an opposing player.

In the Women's National Basketball Association (WNBA), the shot clock doesn't automatically reset to **24 seconds** if the offensive team misses. If they miss but get the ball back, the clock resets to **14 seconds**. It's an incentive to shoot accurately the first time!

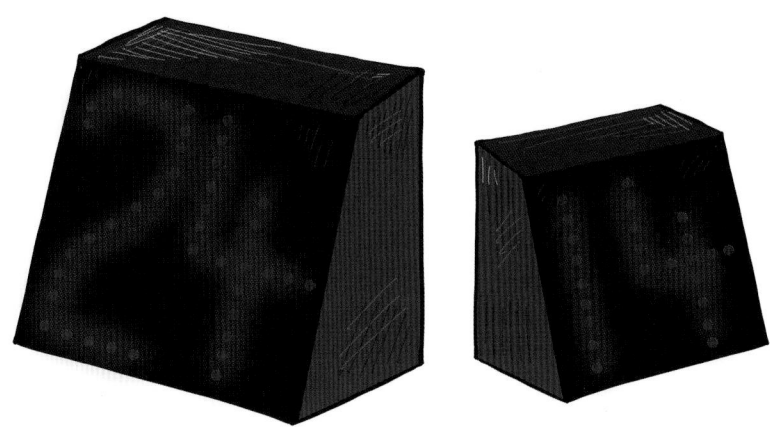

1 – 2 – 3!

The point value for a basket changes depending on the type of shot or how the player makes it. The rules have changed over time.

1

3

2

Baskets were all originally worth a point. But Naismith liked to tinker with his new game, and for a time, he awarded three points for every basket. He finally settled on baskets being worth two points. That was the standard for 70 years.

But shots from *really* far away can be harder to make, so in the 1960s, the American Basketball Association (the ABA, a rival league to the NBA) introduced the idea of making these shots worth more—three points. The idea caught on quickly at every level of the game—except in the NBA. Those in charge thought the new system was a gimmick and didn't accept the three-point shot till 1979.

CROSS THE LINE

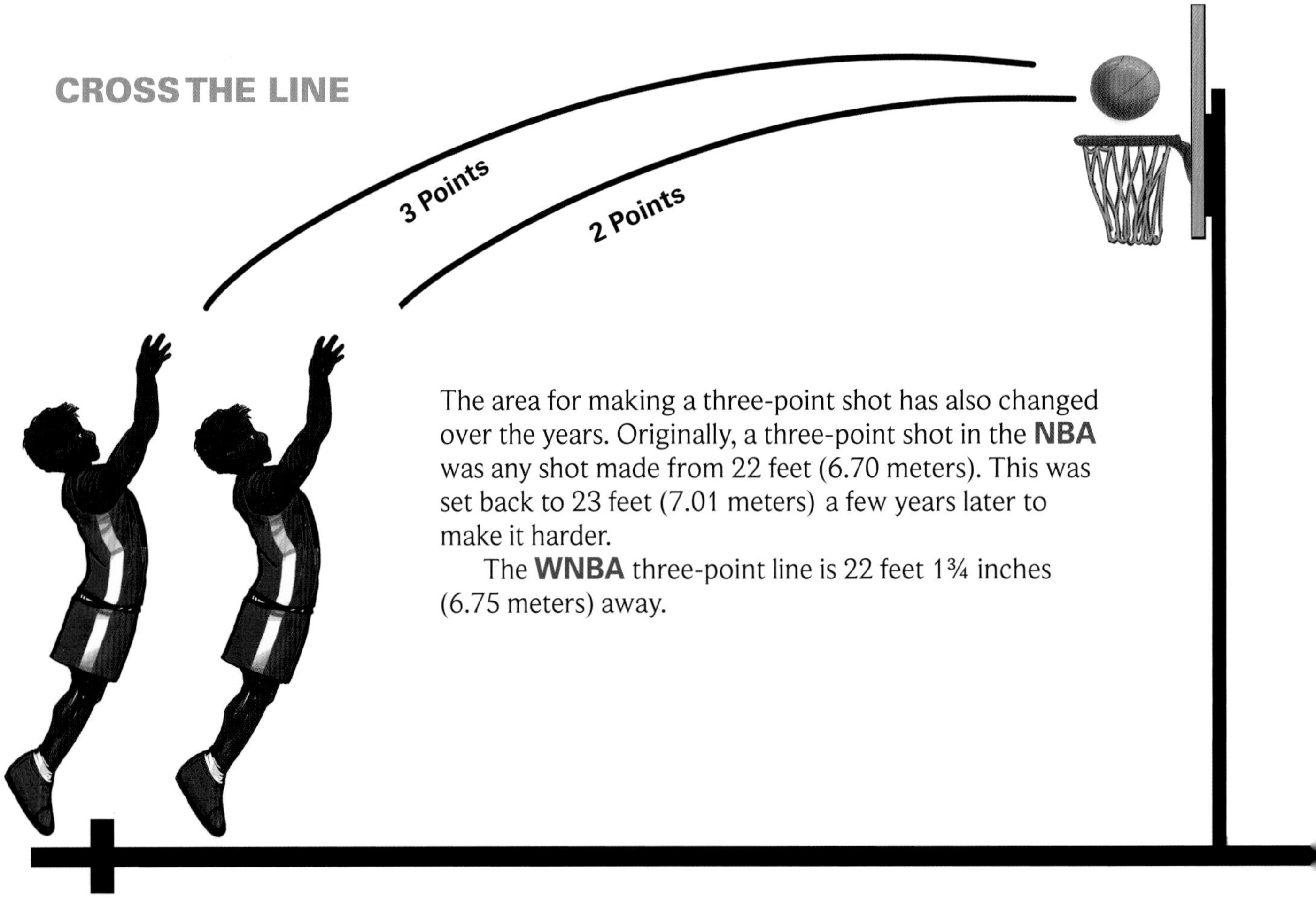

3 Points

2 Points

The area for making a three-point shot has also changed over the years. Originally, a three-point shot in the **NBA** was any shot made from 22 feet (6.70 meters). This was set back to 23 feet (7.01 meters) a few years later to make it harder.

The **WNBA** three-point line is 22 feet 1¾ inches (6.75 meters) away.

A shot is worth more on the far side of the line.

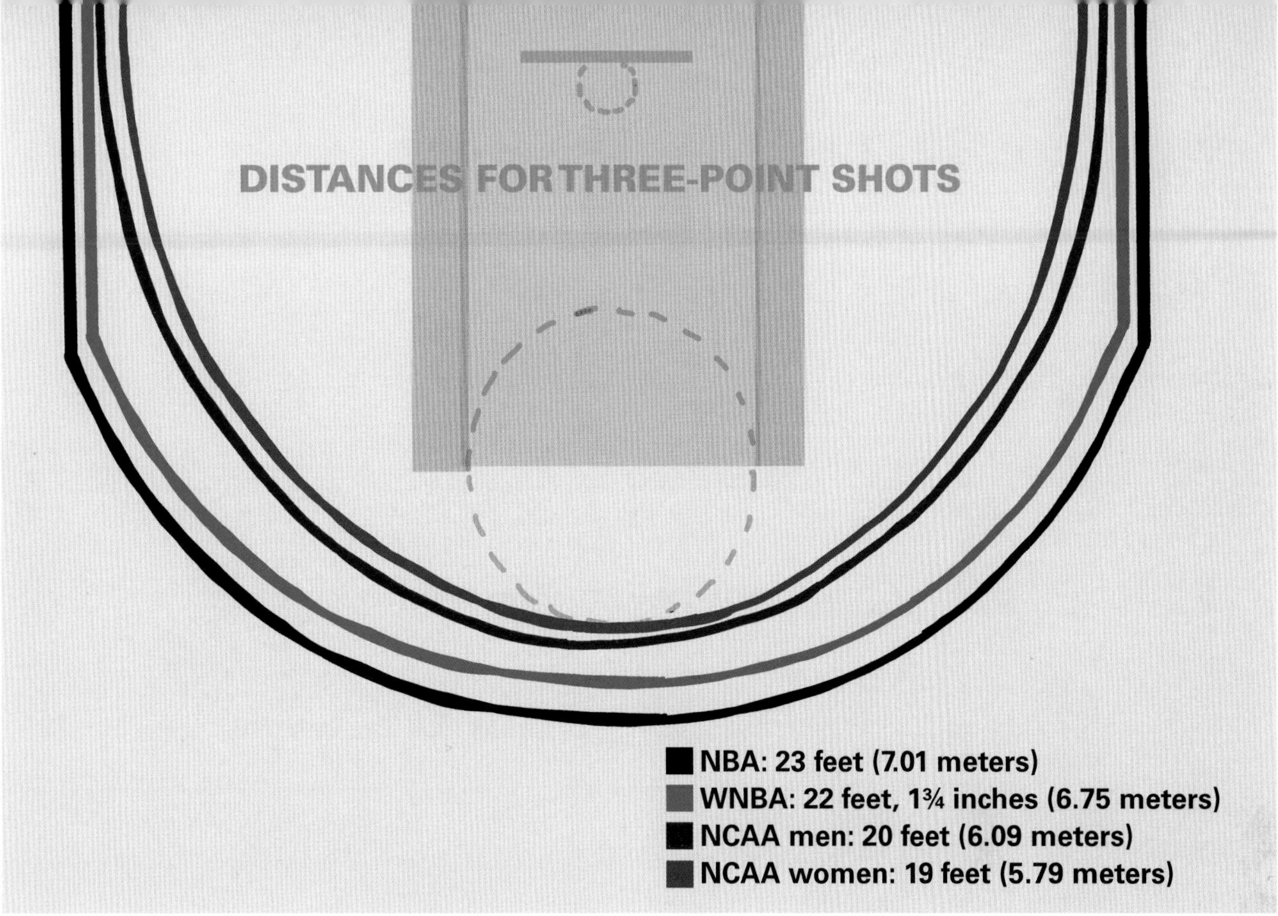

DISTANCES FOR THREE-POINT SHOTS

■ **NBA: 23 feet (7.01 meters)**
■ **WNBA: 22 feet, 1¾ inches (6.75 meters)**
■ **NCAA men: 20 feet (6.09 meters)**
■ **NCAA women: 19 feet (5.79 meters)**

NO GOALIE ALLOWED

Little-known fact: you can score two or three points without scoring a basket. How? Early on, tall players would sometimes just stand by the basket and swat shots away as they fell toward the hoop—like a goalie in soccer or hockey. This seemed against the spirit of the game, so in the 1940s, most leagues banned the practice. Now, if a player swats a ball that's headed down toward the basket, it counts as an automatic two or three points (depending on where the shot came from) for the shooting team.

THE FREE THROW

Naismith didn't mention foul shots in the original rules, but he soon added them to make the game more fair, and more interesting.

Naismith originally awarded one free point to a team every time its opponent committed three fouls. But then, he decided it would be more fun to make a team shoot to earn the points—the "free throw," worth a point each.

Free throws are taken from the foul line, 15 feet (4.57 meters) from the hoop, with no one trying to block you. It seems easy, but the best team in the NBA still misses an average of 20% of their free throws. Ben Wallace missed more than *half* the free throws he took in his career.

Maybe it's the nerves. Maybe it's the pressure of all those people watching you.

The best NBA team hits 80%

Ben Wallace only made 50%

Ted St. Martin isn't an NBA player, but he has made free throws his obsession. He once made 5,221 in a row. It took him 7 hours and 20 minutes! He's actually broken his own record 15 times and now helps train other players. His secret? He says it's practice.

"HEY, LOOK AT THIS!"

Hometown fans do everything from waving Styrofoam noodles to booing loudly to distract an opposing player during a free throw. The fans at Arizona State have a "curtain of distraction." This is an actual curtain set up near the opposing team's hoop. Just as a shooter gets ready to let go of the ball, students open the curtain. They've revealed everything from dancing unicorns to US Olympic swimmer Michael Phelps dressed in a Speedo and wearing all his gold medals! And it works! Stats suggest that opposing players are missing, on average, about 10% more foul shots at Arizona State than anywhere else.

WHAT WOULD *YOU* DO?

There is an almost surefire way to make more free throws, but hardly anyone wants to do it.

Rick Barry was one of the greatest free-throw shooters of all time. He credited practice and his technique.

90%

Barry threw the ball underhand. It was easier to aim, he said, because you steadied the ball with both hands before releasing it. You also threw the ball with less force, so if you didn't shoot perfectly the rebound would be softer than from a ball thrown overhand. So the chances were higher that it would go in. Barry made nearly *90%* of his free throws over his 15-year career.

For years, he tried to convince more players to shoot this way. He would always quote the stats. But almost no one ever agreed to try.

OVERHAND SUPERSTARS

This isn't to say you *have* to shoot underhand to be accurate. Elena Delle Donne made 93.9% of her shots over 77 games from 2013 to 2015—almost equal to a full NBA season. Peja Stojakovic made 92.7% over 81 games in the 2003/04 season. Of course, Barry is next on the list with a 92.4% average in 1977/78.

SHOTS

50%

overhand

Why? It's not the math; it's psychology. For example, in his record-setting 100-point game in 1962, Wilt Chamberlain scored 28 of 32 free-throw attempts by throwing underhand. He had a 61% average for free throws in that season—you guessed it, throwing underhand.

But he soon switched back to overhand throwing, and was notoriously bad at it—making more like 45–50% of his shots. When asked about it, Chamberlain said people made fun of him using a "granny shot," and that he "felt like a sissy."

What would you do if you had the choice?

SHOTS

61%

underhand

THE ARC AND THE ANGLE

The key to hitting a perfect shot is math. Yup—math. So pay attention in class!

When you shoot a basketball, you are actually—although subconsciously—calculating the best arc for the flight of the ball from your hand to the basket. The higher the arc, the better the chance the ball will go in. This is because the available space inside the rim changes depending on the arc of the shot coming in.

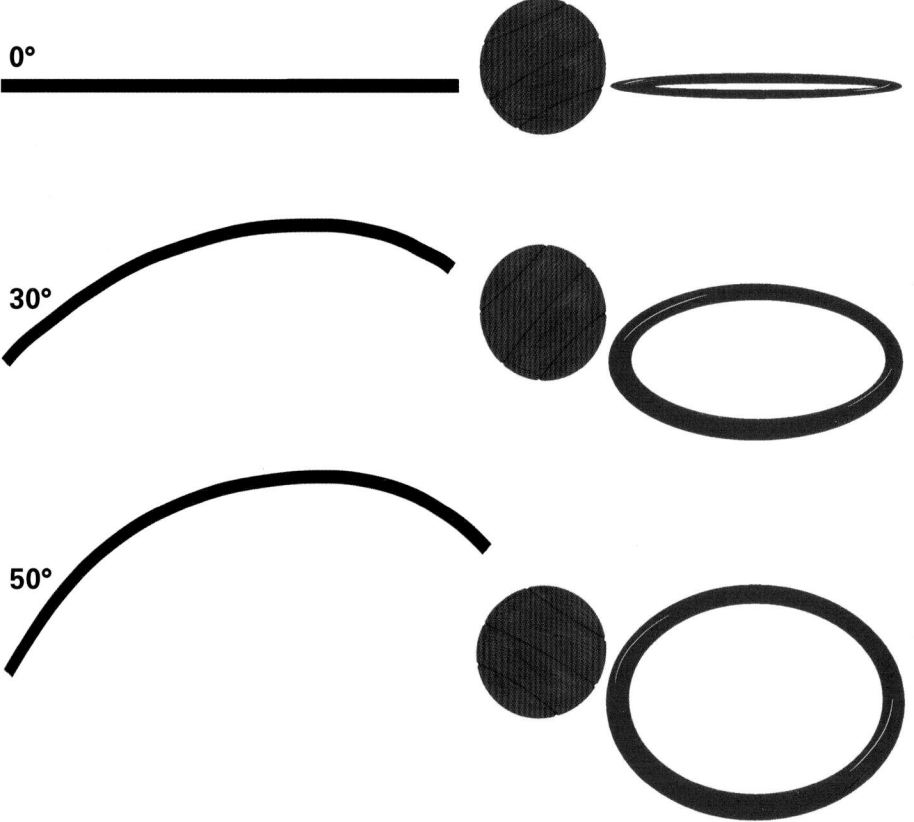

Studies have shown that a 45- to 50-degree arc is the most successful. Why? It's neither straight at the target nor *too* high. The higher the angle, the more force it takes to shoot it.

Try throwing a basketball in a really high arc toward the basket. It takes an incredible amount of energy because you are throwing the ball *upward* as well as *forward*. And it's hard to control the shot when you're so busy concentrating on just getting it that high. The ball also has to travel a longer distance in the air.

So, what you want is something high enough to create a big target, but not so high that it's too difficult a shot to make—about 50 degrees.

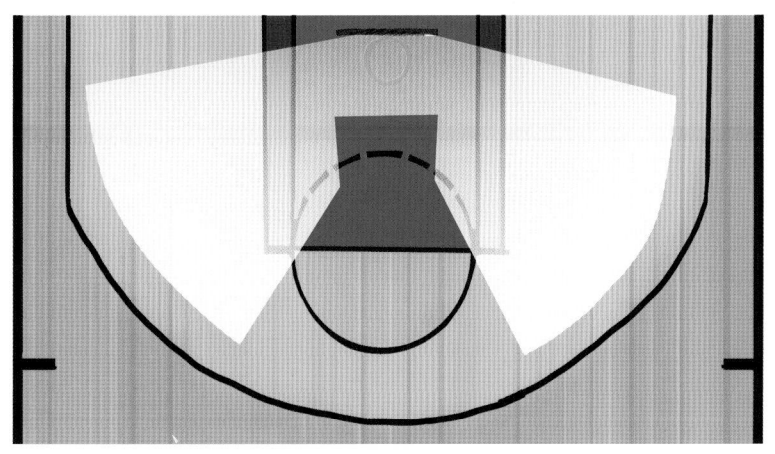

THE ART (AND SCIENCE) OF THE BANK SHOT

Not all shots are taken from far away. Many are bank shots, often close to the basket. With this type of shot, the ball is "banked"—or bounced—off the backboard at an angle that will allow it to pass down and through the net.

A study by researchers at North Carolina State examined more than a million shots and discovered a couple of things. One: there's a zone where it makes more sense to try to angle the ball off the backboard than aiming right at the hoop.

As you move more and more to the side of the basket, the angle you need to aim for on the backboard increases.

This forms an imaginary V on the backboard. Seen from straight on, it looks like this.

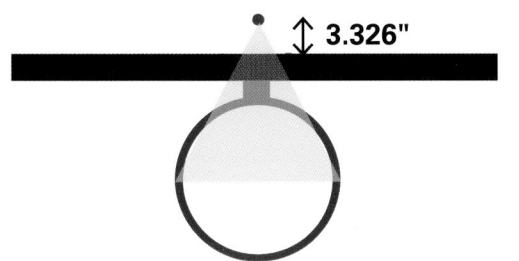

3.326"

But the study found something else cool. The best bank shots are aimed at a spot 3.326 inches (8.4 centimeters) behind the backboard.

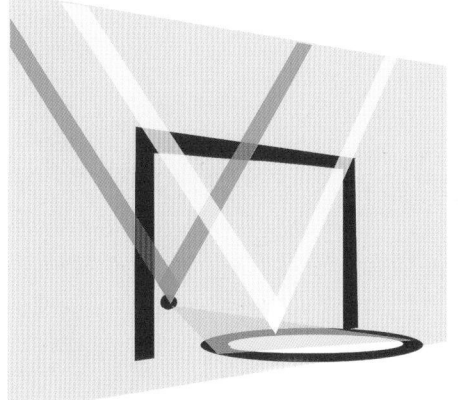

It's like the V moves behind the backboard. There's some art here, too, because you need to throw the ball softly or else it will bounce too far off the backboard. It's Newton's laws of physics in action—the more force you put into the ball, the more it bounces. (Oh, yeah, pay attention in science, too!)

Putting spin on the ball also helps, because the spin creates friction with the backboard, which actually takes some of the force away from the ball.

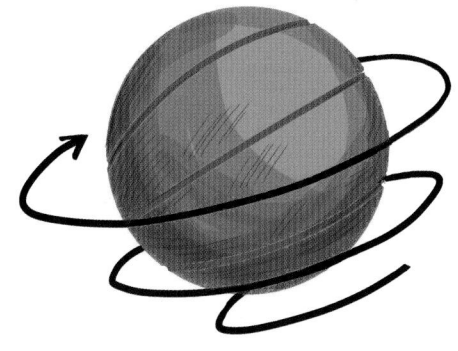

SLAM DUNK!

There's one way to forget about arcs and angles (and math and science!) altogether—by stuffing the ball right into the hoop.

There's some debate about who "dunked" first. Joe Fortenberry was a member of the US Olympic team in 1936. He was 6 feet 8 inches (2.03 meters) and could put the ball directly in the net. A writer said it looked just like he was "dunking a roll in coffee."

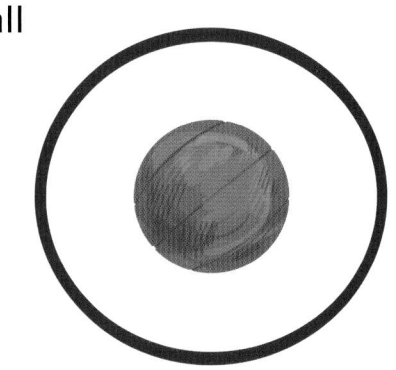

In the 1940s, college star Bob Kurland was 7 feet (2.13 meters) tall and dunked a lot. It wasn't always popular. Opposing players saw the tactic as unsporting and would sometimes try to hurt Kurland.

But as players got bigger and bigger, the practice became more and more accepted. And the fans loved it!

DUNKING IN THE WNBA

In 1984, Georgeann Wells became the first woman to dunk in a college game. The dunk isn't a big part of the WNBA. There have only been about a dozen since the league started. Why? The average height of the players is probably the main reason. On average, WNBA players are 7 inches (almost 18 centimeters) shorter than their NBA counterparts. Brittney Griner is an exception at 6 feet 8 inches (2.03 meters), and she's made almost half the dunks in WNBA history.

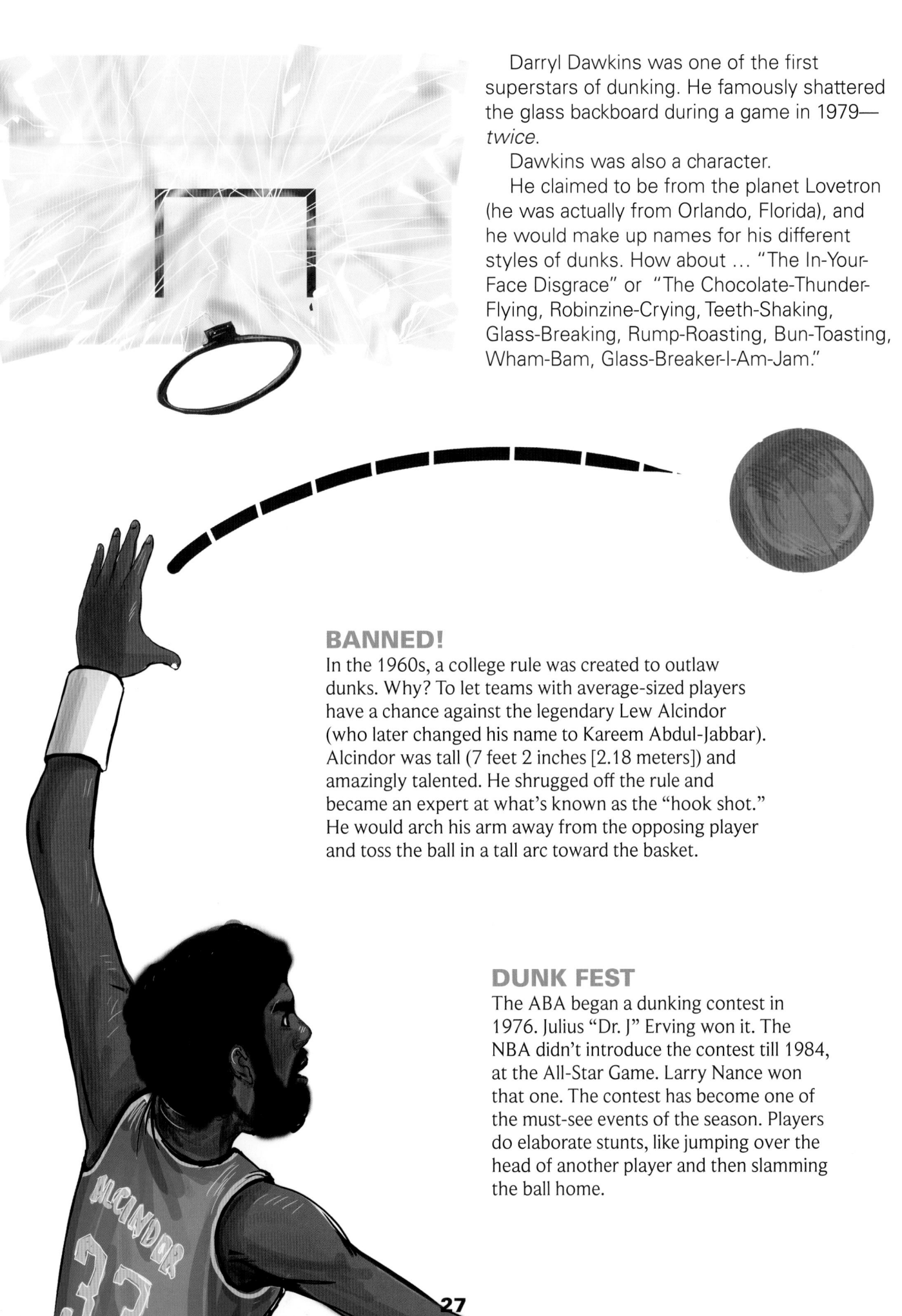

Darryl Dawkins was one of the first superstars of dunking. He famously shattered the glass backboard during a game in 1979—*twice*.

Dawkins was also a character.

He claimed to be from the planet Lovetron (he was actually from Orlando, Florida), and he would make up names for his different styles of dunks. How about … "The In-Your-Face Disgrace" or "The Chocolate-Thunder-Flying, Robinzine-Crying, Teeth-Shaking, Glass-Breaking, Rump-Roasting, Bun-Toasting, Wham-Bam, Glass-Breaker-I-Am-Jam."

BANNED!

In the 1960s, a college rule was created to outlaw dunks. Why? To let teams with average-sized players have a chance against the legendary Lew Alcindor (who later changed his name to Kareem Abdul-Jabbar). Alcindor was tall (7 feet 2 inches [2.18 meters]) and amazingly talented. He shrugged off the rule and became an expert at what's known as the "hook shot." He would arch his arm away from the opposing player and toss the ball in a tall arc toward the basket.

DUNK FEST

The ABA began a dunking contest in 1976. Julius "Dr. J" Erving won it. The NBA didn't introduce the contest till 1984, at the All-Star Game. Larry Nance won that one. The contest has become one of the must-see events of the season. Players do elaborate stunts, like jumping over the head of another player and then slamming the ball home.

FEET FIRSTS

The original basketball shoes were made of thin canvas and rubber. Wow, have things changed.

Chuck Taylor was one of the game's first superstars, and he helped design the "standard" basketball shoe. Almost 100% of players wore these up till the 1970s.

Then, Nike and other companies began making "high-tops," with more ankle support, leather uppers, and cushioned soles. These high-tops also became a huge fashion symbol when an image of superstar Michael Jordan doing his signature "air" jump was featured on the side in 1984.

SHOE PRICES: A BRIEF HISTORY

1910 $1

1950 $4

1980 $20

Today $50+

AIR JORDAN

Michael Jordan got into trouble for wearing his own shoes. Back in the 1980s, the NBA had a strict policy that said all shoes had to be white. Jordan's were a way cooler red and black. He was fined $5,000 for every game in which he wore them. But they became so popular that Nike released a public version the next year. Before long, Nike was the biggest shoe manufacturer in the world.

The shoes cost $65 in 1985. Today, a new pair of Jordans sells for about $300. A pair of original shoes, worn by Jordan himself, recently sold for $70,000!

Vintage shoes have become hot collectors' items. "Sneakerhead" Richard Kosow has paid tens of thousands of dollars for collectible shoes and has thousands of them sealed in an airtight vault. You can see a gallery of them on his website: www.sneakermuseum.com.

These days, basketball shoes are a billion-dollar industry. Michael Jordan shoes still sell more than anyone else's—bringing in more than **$2 billion** worldwide per year!

$2 Billion

LeBron James is the top seller among active players. His brand sales rack up **$300 million** worldwide. (LeBron gets paid about $40 million to endorse products each year—on top of his NBA salary, which is about $33 million.)

$300 Million

INCREDIBLE FEET

Shaquille O'Neal has the largest NBA shoes on record—size 22. (Actually, four other players are tied with Shaq, but he's the most famous.) Kenny George—who only played in college—has the biggest shoe size on record, at size 26. Brittney Griner, who plays for the WNBA, laces up at an impressive men's size 17.

MAGIC!

Here's a neat trick to discover someone's shoe size and their age at the beginning of the year. Find a friend and ask them to write down their shoe size (no half sizes), but not to tell you what it is. Let's say they wear a size 8, they were born in 2000, and the current year is 2017. Ask your friend to

1. multiply their shoe size by 5 ($8 \times 5 = 40$).
2. add 50 to that number ($40 + 50 = 90$).
3. multiply that number by 20 ($90 \times 20 = 1,800$).
4. add 1,016 ($1,800 + 1,016 = 2,816$).
5. subtract the year they were born ($2,816 - 2000 = 816$).

The total is their shoe size (8) plus their age at the beginning of 2017 (16)!

A size 22 shoe isn't 22 inches (55.8 centimeters).
It's actually closer to 16 inches (40.6 centimeters).

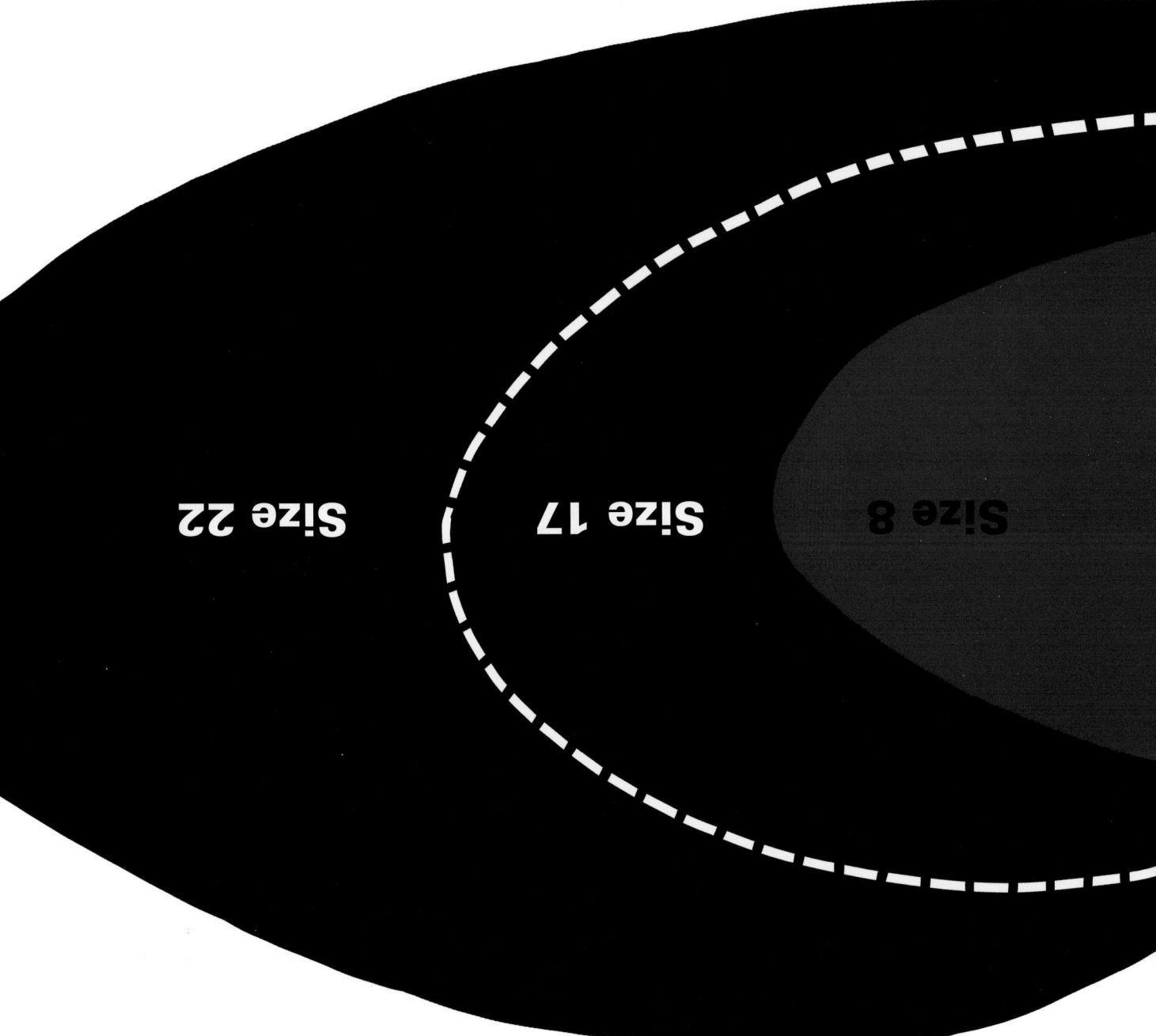

Size 22   Size 17   Size 8

MAGIC EXPLAINED

It's not magic that's at work here, it's algebra. This person provided their shoe size in step 1 (size 8) as well as their year of birth (step 5), which is used to calculate their age. The rest is just a fancy equation that makes sure the answer is the person's shoe size times 100, plus their age at the beginning of the year. (In step 4, you have to make sure the last two digits of the number you add are the last two digits of the year that just ended. So, if last year was 2017, you'd have to add 1,017.) Tricky!

THE COLOR BARRIER

These days, basketball is one of the most diverse sports in the world. But for years, there was a color barrier at the pro level.

Naismith taught the game to white schoolboys. That was the reality of his world in 1891.

It was Edwin B. Henderson, in 1904, who realized the sport would be great for his students in inner-city Washington, DC—many of whom were African-American. Schools there (and almost everywhere at the time) were segregated.

Henderson thought the sport would help raise "vigorous youth" and would also be a tool to promote civil rights, allowing young African-American athletes a chance to show off their mental and physical abilities.

Henderson played for one of the great DC teams, the 12 Streeters. They later became, at his suggestion, the first African-American varsity team—at Howard University.

The sport spread and found an especially fertile home in New York City.

The New York All Stars were the first professional African-American men's team, formed by Major A. Hart in 1910. They played exhibition games against all-white teams. The team folded in 1913, but the idea of all-African-American teams caught hold and more teams formed in the 1920s.

This era became known as the "Black Fives" era. *Five* refers to the number of starting players on a team. The big teams were New York Rens, the Commonwealth Big Five, New York Incorporators, the Loendi Big Five, and the Harlem Globetrotters.

The Rens traveled all over the United States, often facing discrimination even as they played—and beat—white teams. In Indiana, a café owner surrounded their table with a screen so the other customers wouldn't have to see them eat. In other cities, they were refused hotel rooms and would sleep in their bus.

BUCKY LEW

Harry "Bucky" Lew was a notable exception during the time when teams were segregated by color. He was the first African-American player to sign a pro contract—with a YMCA team in 1898. He led the team to a state championship but faced constant racist taunts. "All those things you read about Jackie Robinson, the abuse, the name-calling, extra effort to put him down ... they're all true," he once said. "I got the same treatment and even worse."

Lew barnstormed (traveled for exhibition games) for a few years after he left the YMCA team before retiring to run his family's dry-cleaning business.

African-American women's basketball clubs also sprang up in the New York area: the New York Girls, the Spartan Girls of Brooklyn, and the Jersey Girls.

New York beat New Jersey 12–3 in their very first game.

INTEGRATION

Racial integration took a long time, but once everyone could play pro, the game changed rapidly.

The National Basketball League (NBL) had two mostly African-American teams in 1942—the Toledo Jim White Chevrolets and the Chicago Studebaker Flyers. Both teams folded that year. The NBL merged with the NBA in 1949.

The first African-American player drafted by an NBA team was Chuck Cooper. He was drafted by Boston in 1950. But Earl Lloyd, who was drafted by Washington in a later round of that same draft, was the first to play in an actual game, in October of that year. Cooper made his debut the next day.

The first player to actually sign an NBA contract was Nat "Sweetwater" Clifton, who played for the Harlem Globetrotters before signing with the New York Knicks, also in 1950.

This was great for the players, but not so much for the African-American leagues, which folded soon after.

THE HARLEM GLOBETROTTERS
The Harlem Globetrotters survived the collapse of the African-American pro leagues by becoming a traveling theatrical all-star show. They still travel the world showing off incredible dunks, spins, dribbles, and hidden-ball tricks (they would actually hide the ball in the backs of their jerseys and run to the hoop). They even gave Wilt Chamberlain his first pro gig. He later went on to become one of the NBA's all-time greats.

MAKEUP OF NBA ROSTERS

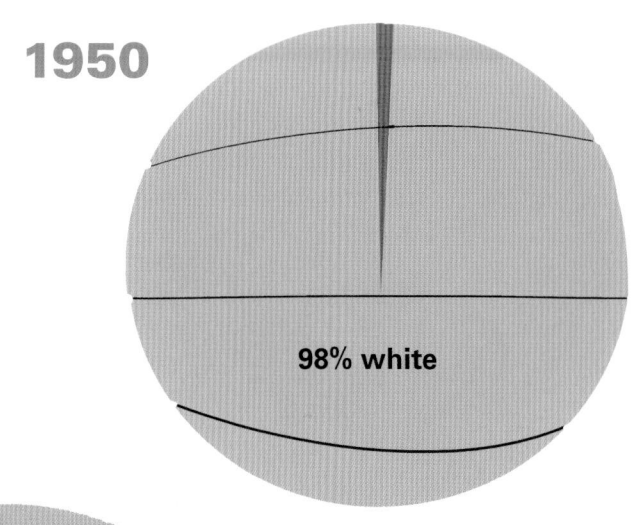

1950

2% African-American

98% white

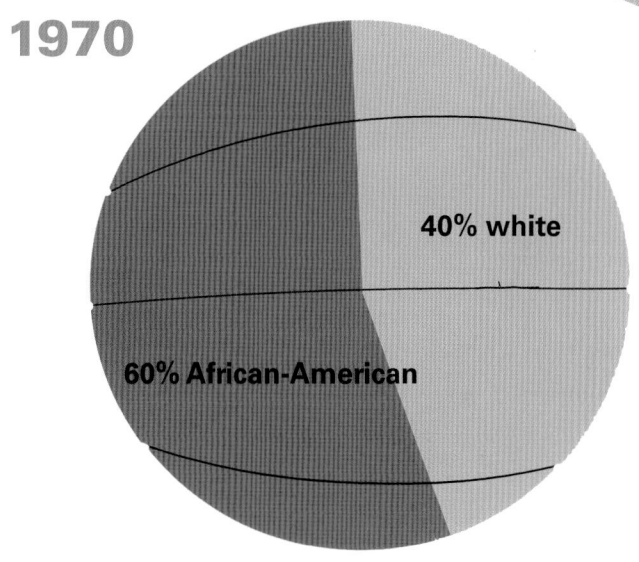

1970

40% white

60% African-American

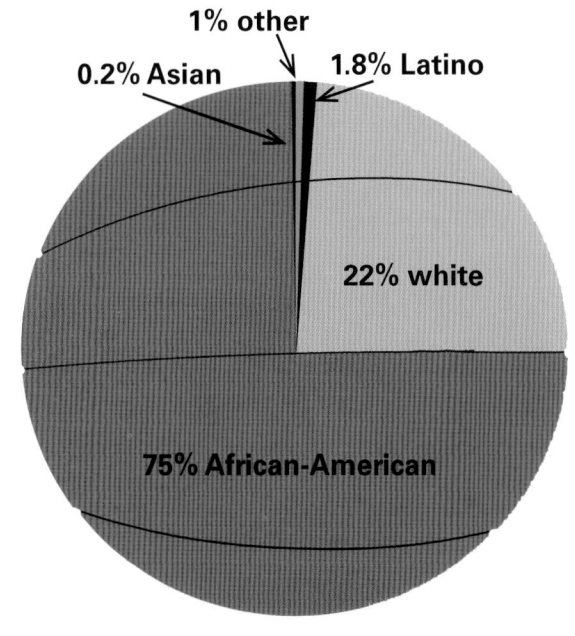

2016

1% other

0.2% Asian

1.8% Latino

22% white

75% African-American

Japanese-American Wataru Misaka played in the NBA in 1947/48.

THE WOMEN'S GAME IS BORN

As we've seen, women have played the game almost as long as men.

Senda Berenson heard about the game *one month* after it was created and introduced it to the girls at her nearby school—Smith College.

For the first few years, the women at Smith played according to Naismith's rules, but then Berenson made some tweaks. Back then, women were still thought of as "the weaker sex," and she felt the game had "a tendency to roughness." So, she divided the court into three zones, and players were not allowed to move from their area. Not a *huge* change, but pretty big.

Berenson established her new rules in 1899, and they stayed the standard for the women's game for more than 60 years.

THE MOTHER OF BASKETBALL

Senda Berenson is often called the "mother of basketball." She had been a sickly child and avoided exercise. Some days, she was too ill to attend school or play piano (her first love). But as an adult, she enrolled in a school that offered physical education. She went from weak and tired to strong and energetic, and she became a huge supporter of sports for women.

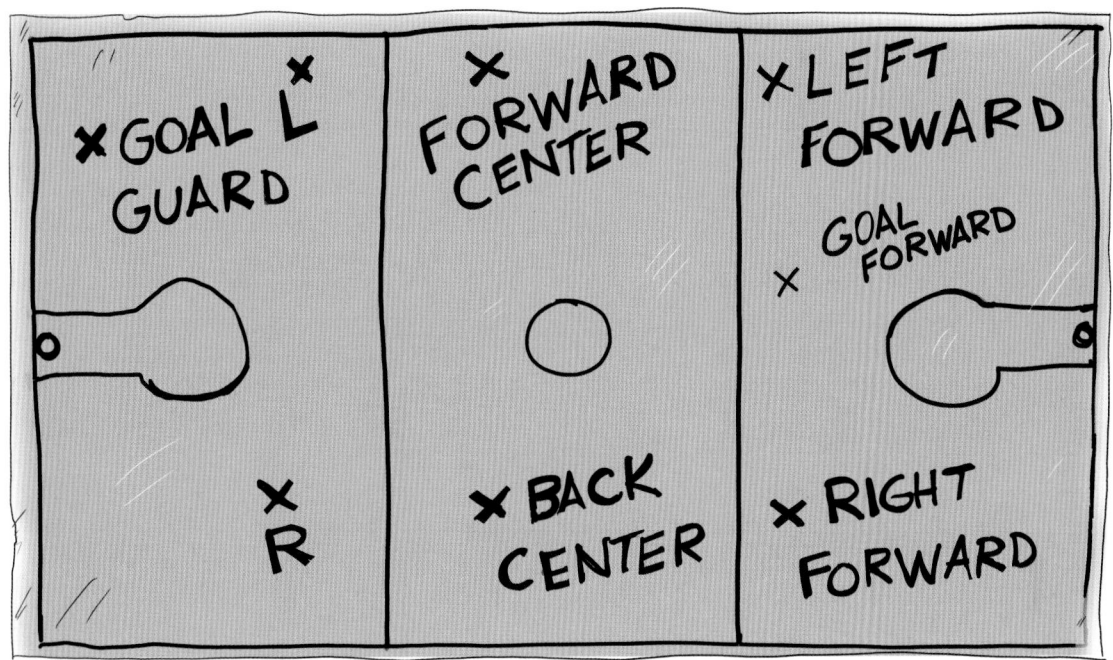

Senda Berenson's book *Basket Ball for Women,* published in 1901—with hand-drawn schematics—helped spread the game even more.

THE RED HEADS

Women made up one of the first barnstorming (touring) teams—the All American Red Heads. They formed in 1936, played men's teams (using men's rules), and won a lot. In 1940, they were the first pro team to play in the Philippines. Why Red Heads? The original owner's wife ran a salon—and all the players had great red hair, either dyed or naturally!

Hazel Walker played with the Red Heads for a short time. Then, she decided to start her own team, the Arkansas Travelers. This made her the first woman to *own* a professional team.

WOMEN GO PRO

In 1996, the women's game went pro with the formation of the Women's National Basketball Association (WNBA).

There were eight teams in 1997, when the league's first official game was played. The Houston Comets won the first four championships, and then folded a few years later. Minnesota and Phoenix have won three titles each.

There are currently 12 WNBA teams: Atlanta, Chicago, Connecticut, Dallas, Indiana, Los Angeles, New York, Minnesota, Phoenix, San Antonio, Seattle, and Washington, DC.

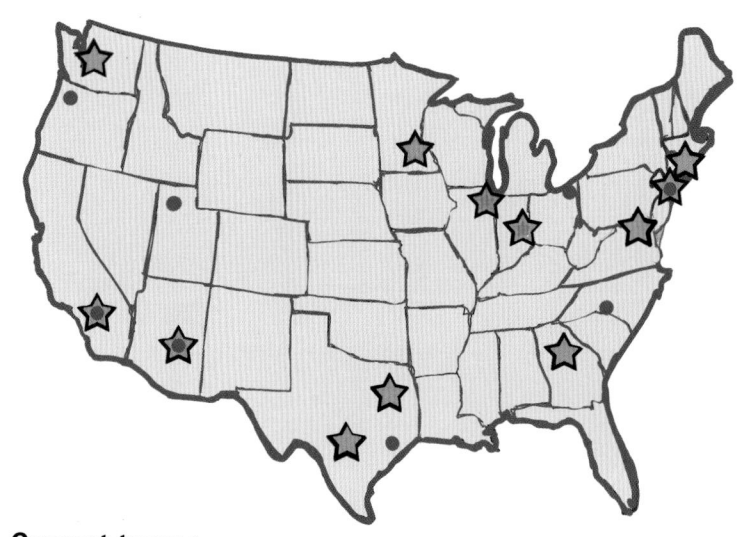

⭐ **Current teams**

● **1997**

The balls are slightly smaller than the NBA balls (by about an inch in circumference), and their season is shorter (only 34 games instead of 82, played from May to September, and followed by the play-offs), but otherwise the game is essentially the same.

Half of the 12 head coaches and about a quarter of the 30 referees are women.

SWOOPES!

The awesomely named Sheryl Swoopes was the first player to be signed to the WNBA (by Houston) and the first superstar of the league. She'd been a record-setting player in college, and that continued in the WNBA.

She gave birth to her son just before the first WNBA season started and was back on the court just six weeks later. She also won three Olympic gold medals with the US team and was the first woman to have her own Nike shoe—the Air Swoopes.

Swoopes was named the most valuable player three times and won four titles.

WOMEN IN CHARGE

In 2006, Violet Palmer became the first female official to work in the NBA. She and Lauren Holtkamp are the only female NBA officials. There are about 70 male officials.

The NBA also has two women assistant coaches. Becky Hammon is an assistant coach with the San Antonio Spurs. She's also the first woman to be a head coach in the NBA's summer league. She won the title that year as well.

Nancy Lieberman is an assistant coach with the Sacramento Kings. She was also the first woman to play on a men's pro team when she signed with Springfield of the United States Basketball League (USBL) in 1986.

How does this compare to other sports? Kathryn Smith is the only full-time coach in the National Football League (NFL). She's with Buffalo. The National Hockey League's Arizona Coyotes hired Dawn Braid as their full-time skating coach. She works with the team in practice but not during games.

Major league baseball doesn't have any.

TITLE IX

You may not have heard about Title IX (Nine), but you should. It has revolutionized the world of sports.

Title IX is a law in the United States that was passed in 1972, and it paved the way for the growth in women's sports. The law ordered high schools and colleges to end discrimination based on gender for any programs that are supported by federal money.

Title IX doesn't just apply to sports, but that's where it has had the biggest impact. The bottom line is that any school that has men's sports has to provide "equivalent" funding for women's sports. There are some exceptions (like football), but the result has been that women's sports have exploded in US colleges.

HIGH SCHOOL ATHLETES

Before Title IX

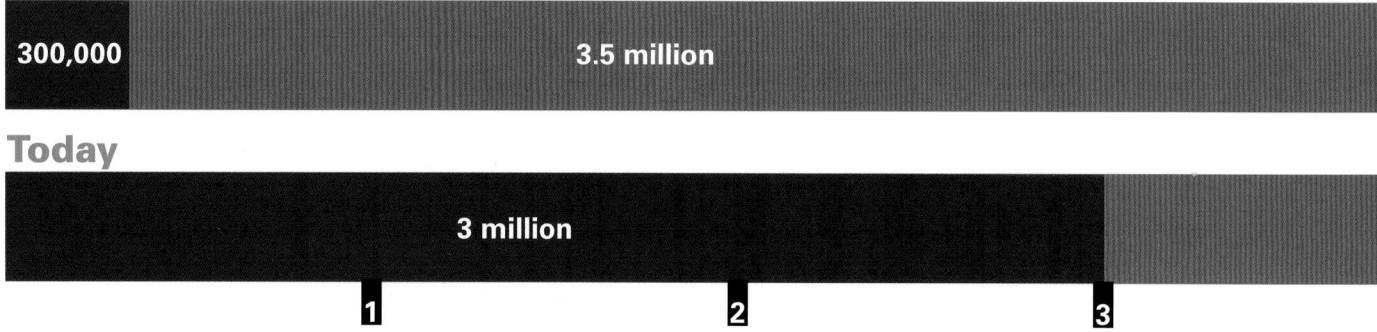

300,000

3.5 million

Today

3 million

1   2   3

Since Title IX, the number of female high school athletes has gone from 300,000 to 3 million—a 900% increase. For boys it's gone from 3.5 million to about 4.5 million, or about a 28% increase.

COLLEGE ATHLETES

Before Title IX

Today

Before Title IX, there were about 30,000 women playing college sports. Today, that number is more like 200,000. That's a rise of about 600%. For the men, there were about 180,000 before Title IX and 250,000 now—a rise of about 40%.

 Women    Men

GETTING IT DONE

In the 1960s, Bernice "Bunny" Sandler had been repeatedly turned down for jobs as a professor. She was told that she "came on too strong for a woman" and that she was not a professor but "just a housewife who went back to school." Furious, she began researching federal laws and uncovered a clause that banned discrimination for any contract that included federal money. She filed complaints against schools that received federal money. Politicians Edith Green and Patsy Mink joined the fight, and Title IX was the result.

Not everything is equal. Men's teams still receive most of the scholarships (about 60%) and control most of the coaching and administrative jobs.

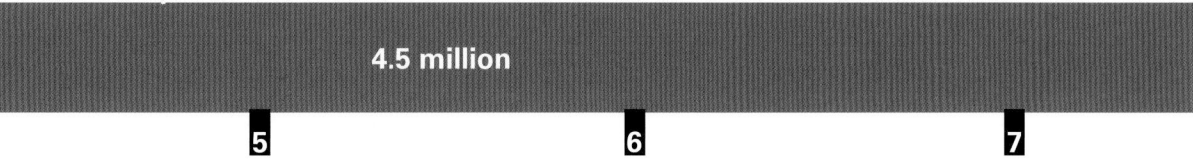

4.5 million

5   6   7

COACHING EQUALITY? WOMEN AND MEN'S TEAMS

Women only coach about 40% of women's teams.

Women only coach about 3% of men's teams.

GLOBE-TROTTING

Basketball wasn't just a huge success at home; it spread around the globe like wildfire.

Almost immediately after it started, the sport became global. This was partially thanks to the fact that Naismith published the rules in 1892 in the YMCA journal *The Triangle*. The YMCA had houses and gyms pretty much everywhere.

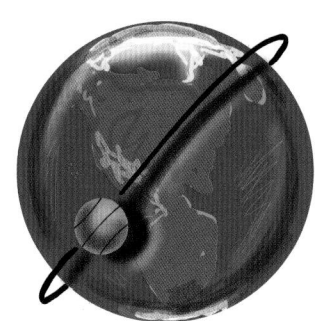

Naismith's fellow Canadians began to play the game in 1892. France started a year later. England hosted its first game in 1894. By the turn of the century, the game had spread to China, India, Japan, and beyond.

The women's game spread around the world just as quickly. There is some evidence that Australia hosted a women's game in 1897, in Victoria. The first world championships were held in 1953 in Chile. (This was only three years after the first men's championship was hosted by, and won by, Argentina).

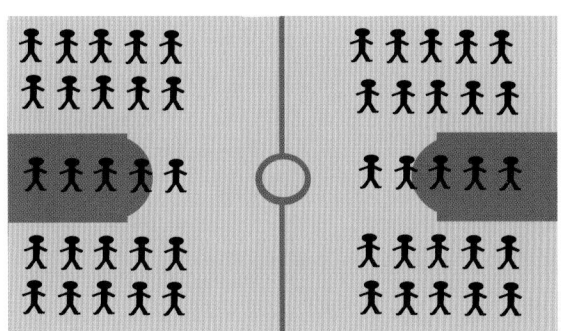 

All of this growth actually had an unintended consequence. The game became so popular that the YMCA had to outlaw it in many countries. Why? Space. Before basketball, gymnastics clubs and other clubs could share the whole gym and fit 50 people in at one time. With basketball, there were only 10 players allowed on the whole court. The YMCA felt basketball players were monopolizing the gym.

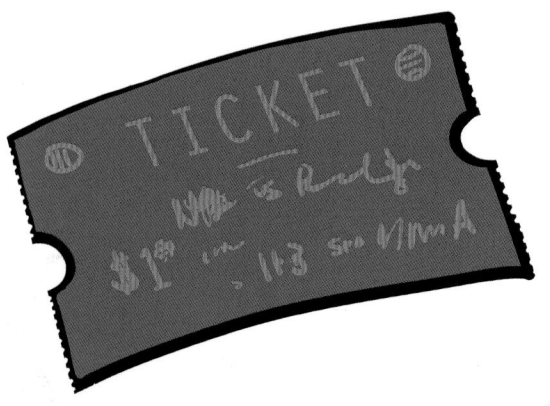

GOING PRO

Basketball players quit the YMCA in protest and began renting private halls where they could play their games. The first "pro" game was held in 1896 in a banquet hall in New Jersey. (Players sold tickets, thus not playing for free.) Trenton, the New Jersey team, beat Brooklyn, 16–1.

Basketball has had international federations for years. The International Basketball Federation (FIBA) was formed in 1932 and governs the sport globally (including in the Philippines, one of the first countries to join—in 1936—thanks to a strong US presence there). FIBA Africa was founded in 1961.

Basketball has also been a huge sport in China for decades. Missionaries introduced the game there soon after Naismith invented it in 1891, and they've had a national league since the 1950s. More recently, Yao Ming, a true superstar in the NBA from 2002 to 2011, helped spread the image of the sport in his home country.

NUMBER OF PLAYERS WORLDWIDE BY SPORT (ACCORDING TO INTERNATIONAL SPORTS FEDERATIONS)

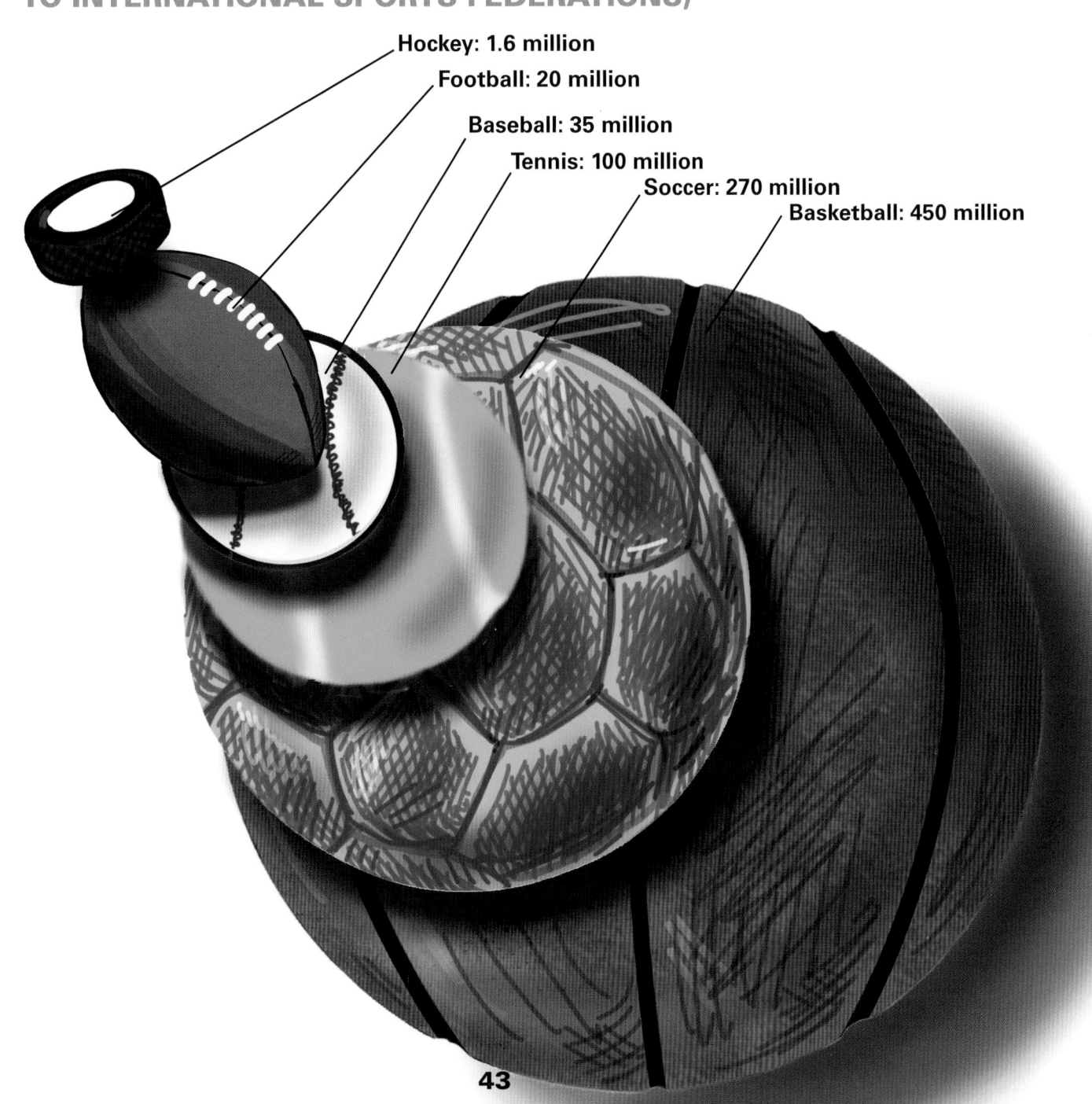

Hockey: 1.6 million

Football: 20 million

Baseball: 35 million

Tennis: 100 million

Soccer: 270 million

Basketball: 450 million

WHO'S FROM WHERE?

Given the sport's popularity, it's no surprise that the pros come from just about everywhere.

NUMBER OF NBA PLAYERS PER COUNTRY (2016 ROSTERS)

There are approximately 390 players in the NBA at any given time—30 teams with 13 players each. In both 2015 and 2016, at least 100 of them were from more than 35 countries outside the United States.

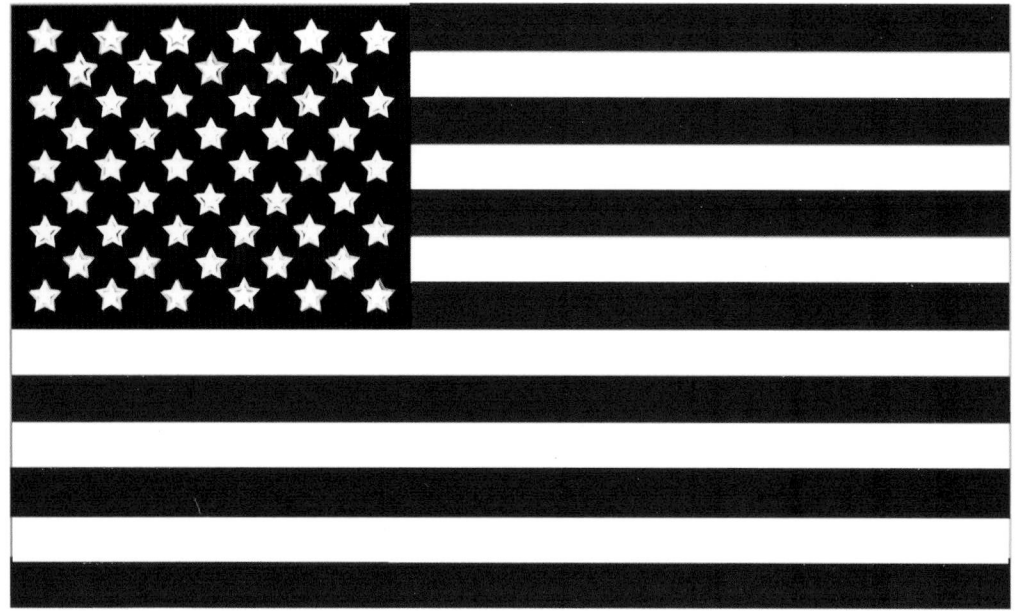

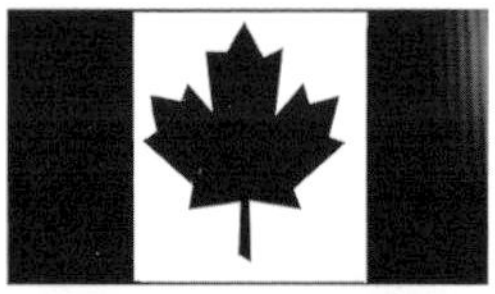

11: Canada

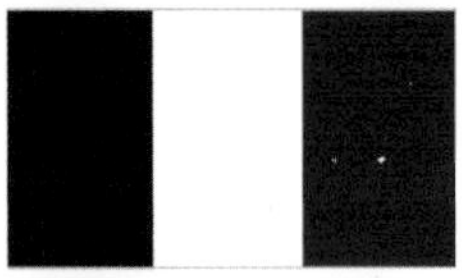

10: France

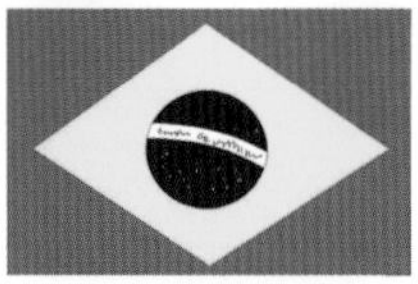

9: Brazil

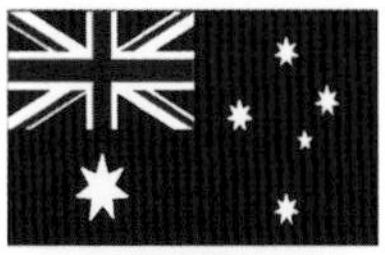

8: Australia

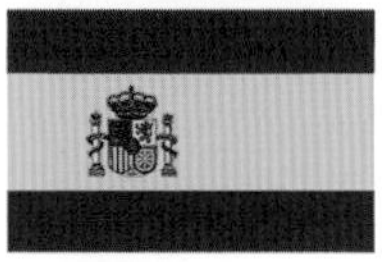

8: Spain

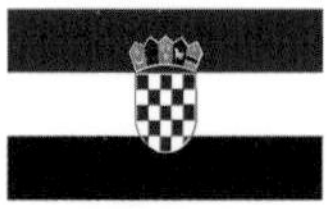

5: Croatia

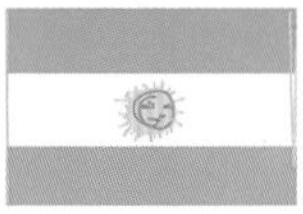

4: Argentina

3

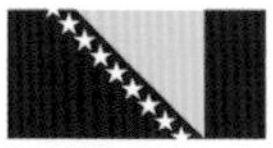

Bosnia and Herzegovina

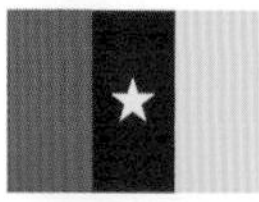

Cameroon

Germany

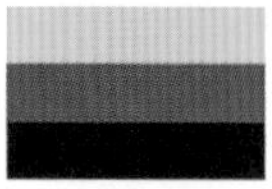

Lithuania

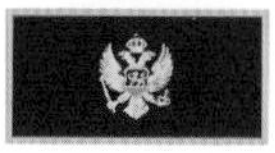

Montenegro

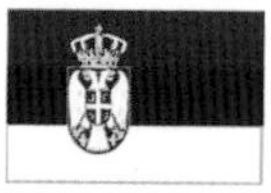

Serbia

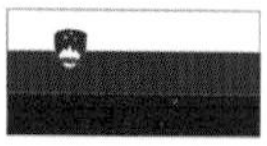

Slovenia

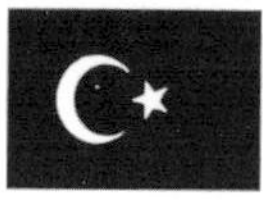

Turkey

2

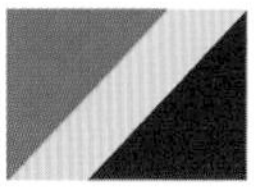

Congo

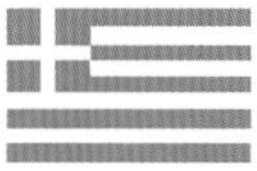

Greece

Italy

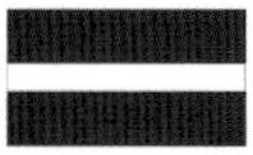

Latvia

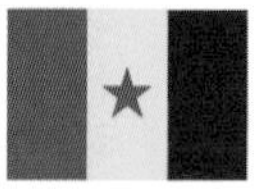

Senegal

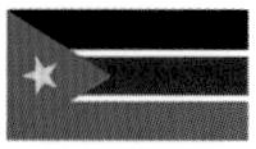

South Sudan

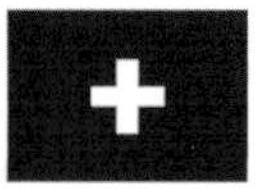

Switzerland

1

◤	Bahamas
	Cape Verde
	Congo
	Czech Republic
	Dominican Republic
	Georgia
	Haiti
	Israel
	Nigeria
	New Zealand
	Poland
	Puerto Rico
	Russia
	Sweden
	Tunisia
	Ukraine
	Venezuela

NUMBER OF WNBA PLAYERS PER COUNTRY (2016 ROSTERS)

In the WNBA, there are 144 players at any given time—12 teams with 12 players each. In 2016, 14 players were from outside the United States.

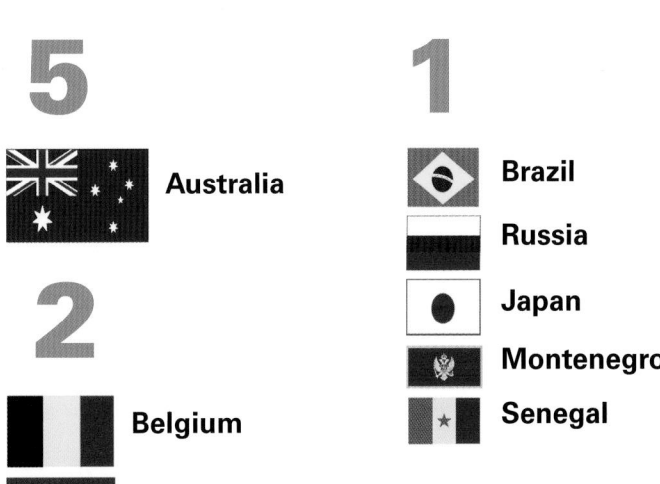

5

	Australia

2

	Belgium
	Serbia

1

	Brazil
	Russia
	Japan
	Montenegro
	Senegal

OLYMPIC ACTION

Basketball was played as a demonstration sport at the 1904 and 1924 Olympic Games. It became an official Olympic sport at the 1936 games in Berlin. Basketball was still mostly American at that point, so the Germans hosted the tournament on tennis courts! Outdoors! James Naismith was on hand to give the medals to the winning teams. The United States won gold, and Canada finished second.

The United States didn't lose a game till 1968—and didn't lose a gold medal till 1972, in a controversial loss to the USSR. Other international Olympic winners were Yugoslavia in 1980 (thanks to a US boycott of the games) and Argentina in 2004.

Women's basketball has been part of the Olympics since 1976—20 years before soccer was included and 22 years before hockey.

THE STREET GAME

Why are there so many basketball players? Just look around your 'hood for the answer.

No matter where you live, it seems every school and park has a basketball court.

Inner-city neighborhoods without the space for a football or baseball field can almost always find room for a court and a couple of hoops. Aside from a ball, no special equipment is needed to play basketball. Below are some approximate prices you might pay to play.

Basketball rim	**$40**
Official basketball	**$40**
A good basketball	**$20**

Hockey net	**$100**
Sticks, pucks, and equipment	**$1,000**
Rink rental	**$150 per hour**

Official soccer ball	**$30**
Nets	**$3,000**

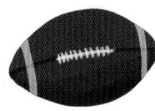

Official football	**$90**
Goalposts	**$9,000**

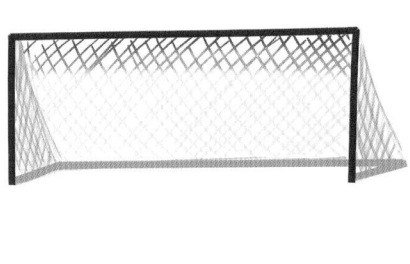

Tennis racquet	**$45**
Balls	**$5 for a pack of three**
Nets	**$300**

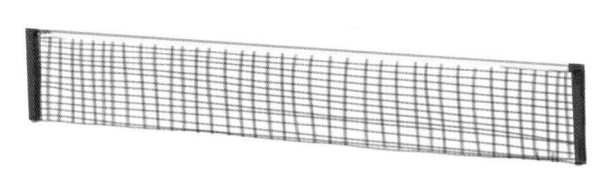

Today, more than 7 million kids aged 6 to 18 play competitive basketball in the United States (slightly more than the number-two sport, soccer), according to the Sports and Fitness Industry Association's Physical Activity Council—and a whole street scene has grown up around the game in North America. Pickup games played on neighborhood courts feature trick shots and blasting music. The hip-hop and rap scenes are intimately tied to the outdoor game, and the street-scene feel has even crept into pro arenas. Games feature nonstop music, and there are now celebrity team owners and superfans, like Jay Z, Rihanna, and Drake.

Of course, those 7 million players mean the odds of making the NBA are incredibly small. Let's assume the best kids make their high school teams. There are about **600,000** kids playing ball at that level right now in North America.

Only **30,000** of those will make it to college ball.

And only **350** of those make it to the NBA. (About 450 different players appear in the NBA each season with about 100 positions taken by athletes from outside of the United States.)

Now look back at the number of players globally (page 43) and think about how tough it is to make the NBA. Want to see that expressed visually? Turn the page.

A DROP OF WATER IN THE OCEAN

This picture is made up of *millions* of tiny dots. Each dot represents one of the millions of people who play basketball. Looks like an idyllic tropical ocean scene!

The basketball-shaped island represents the kids playing ball in North America.

And that one tiny dot in the middle of the ball? It's not a palm tree or a lake.

That's *your* chance of making it to the NBA.

HOPE DREAMS

The dream of making it to the pros can be attractive—especially if it means escaping a rough neighborhood.

The documentary *Hoop Dreams* showed just how attractive that dream can be, and how hard it is to realize. The film followed a pair of talented high school players—Arthur Agee and William Gates—for three years. Both were from underprivileged families in Chicago, and both showed promise of future stardom. But neither player made the NBA. The movie showed just how much they and their families sacrificed, and how incredibly competitive—and ruthless—the sports world can be.

GROWING ... UP!

People have gotten taller since basketball was invented, but basketball players have gotten *much* taller.

The average height for an NBA player in 1950 was 6 feet 2 inches (1.87 meters).

The average NBA player today is closer to 6 feet 6 inches (1.98 meters).

The average height for a North American male today is 5 feet 10 inches (1.78 meters).

180 (81.64)

220 (99.79)

195 (88.45)

Basketball players haven't just gotten taller, they've also gotten heavier. This has changed the style of the game, with more players such as Shaquille O'Neal and LeBron James using their height *and* bulk to smash their way to the net.

Margo Dydek was the tallest WNBA player of all time, at 7 feet 2 inches (2.18 meters). She played in the WNBA from 1998 to 2008.

RAISING THE RIM?

From time to time, there is talk of raising the hoop to 12 feet (3.65 meters) so taller players will rely on the dunk less often. But Wilt Chamberlain, Michael Wilson, Robertas Javtokas, and others have dunked on 12-foot baskets during basketball exhibitions. Dwight Howard even did it wearing a Superman cape at the 2009 All-Star Game.

The average WNBA player is just under 6 feet (1.82 meters).

The average height for a North American woman today is 5 feet 3 inches (1.60 meters).

169 (76.1)   222 (101)   166 (75.3)

TALLEST AND SHORTEST

The tallest player in NBA history is either Gheorghe Muresan or Manute Bol. The NBA lists both players at 7 feet 7 inches (2.31 meters), but *Guinness World Records* gives Muresan a *tiny* advantage.

The shortest is Muggsy Bogues. He is 5 feet 3 inches (1.60 meters).

Bogues and Bol actually played together for Washington in 1987/88.

BIG BUCKS

Just as in other pro sports, basketball has seen a huge rise in player salaries.

The average salary for a player in the first years of the NBA was just a few thousand dollars a year. Now, the base salary for a rookie is half a million.

Here are some notable stars and what they earned in their highest-paid season:

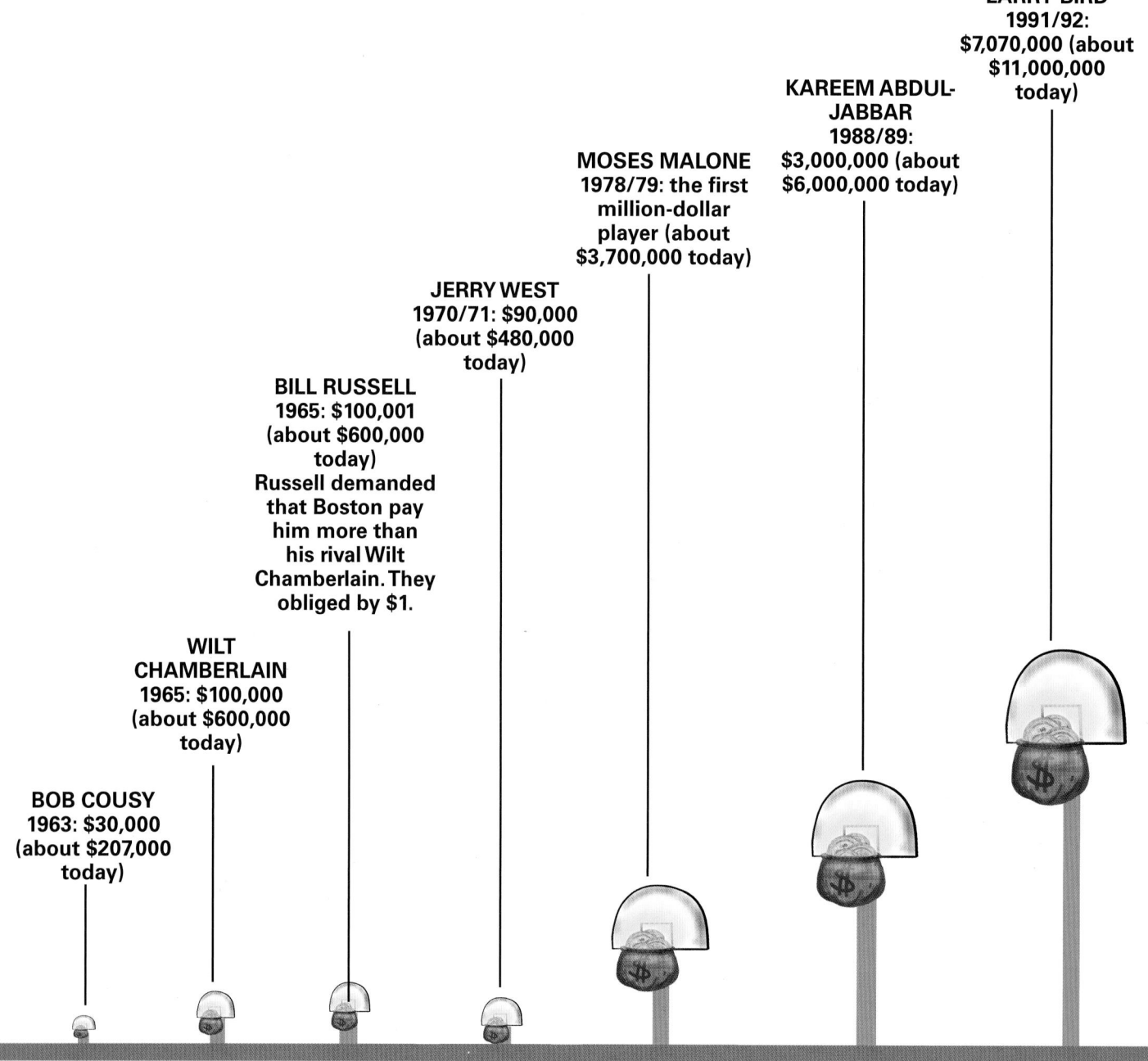

LARRY BIRD
1991/92:
$7,070,000 (about
$11,000,000
today)

KAREEM ABDUL-JABBAR
1988/89:
$3,000,000 (about
$6,000,000 today)

MOSES MALONE
1978/79: the first
million-dollar
player (about
$3,700,000 today)

JERRY WEST
1970/71: $90,000
(about $480,000
today)

BILL RUSSELL
1965: $100,001
(about $600,000
today)
Russell demanded
that Boston pay
him more than
his rival Wilt
Chamberlain. They
obliged by $1.

WILT CHAMBERLAIN
1965: $100,000
(about $600,000
today)

BOB COUSY
1963: $30,000
(about $207,000
today)

ALL-TIME HIGH

LEBRON JAMES 2017: James starts a three-year deal with Cleveland worth $100,000,000—or a little more than $33,000,000 a season.

MICHAEL JORDAN 1997/98: $33,140,000 (about $45,000,000 today)

MUSICAL MONEY

When it comes to money, things have changed—a lot. Back in the beginning, players often needed other jobs to make ends meet. Tony Lavelli played for Boston in the 1960s—and had a bonus in his contract. He got paid an extra $125 to play his accordion at half-time!

The top salary in the **WNBA**, by comparison, is just $109,500—and is earned by a number of players. The organization puts a strict limit on salaries. The total salary allocated for a team is just over $900,000.

Why? The season is shorter, so there are fewer tickets to sell. And the women's game isn't as popular as the men's, so the sources for making money (advertising revenue, TV rights, and merchandising) are also lower than the men's game.

HAIR-RAISING SUPERSTARS

Athletes in hockey, football, and baseball cover their heads with hats or helmets. In basketball, players' heads are naked. Maybe this is why the sport seems to attract some interesting personalities with some awesome hairdos.

Dr. J

Michael Jordan

James Harden

Bill Walton

Chris Andersen

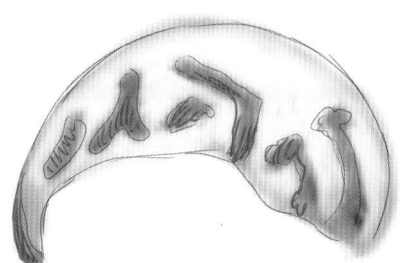

Metta World Peace

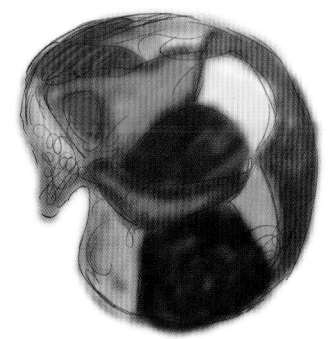

Dennis Rodman

Skylar Diggins

Allen Iverson

Basketball has seen its fair share of characters—and it wasn't just their hair that set them apart.

Dennis Rodman has done everything from marrying himself (in 1996) to visiting North Korea to play basketball for dictator Kim Jong-un (in 2014).

Bill Walton didn't just like sweatbands—he *loved* the Grateful Dead. Walton would spend his free time following the band around the country. He saw the Dead more than *850* times. They even invited him onstage in 1978 to play drums!

Metta World Peace was given the name Ron Artest when he was born. He changed it in 2011 to, in his words, "inspire and bring youth together all around the world." Prior to that, in 2004, Artest had been involved in one of the biggest brawls in sports history, involving players from both teams as well as fans. He was suspended for 86 games, the longest penalty of its kind in NBA history.

And Michael Jordan is sometimes credited with making "bald" a cool look at a time when men were often ashamed to show they were losing their hair.

Brittney Griner

FOR THE RECORD BOOKS— PLAYERS

Some basketball records seem almost unbelievable. But believe them. They're true!

100

Wilt Chamberlain scored **100 points** in a single game. He did it in a 1962 Philadelphia win, **169–147**, against the New York Knicks.*

*Al Attles was the second leading scorer for Philly in that game. He had **17 points**.

81

In 2006, Kobe Bryant scored **81 points** for the Lakers in a **122–104** win over the Toronto Raptors.

51 48

MOST POINTS IN A WNBA GAME
Riquna Williams: **51** on September 8, 2013
Maya Moore: **48** on July 22, 2014

MOST FOULS
Darryl Dawkins: 386 (1983/84)
Darryl, again: 379 (1982/83)
Steve Johnson: 372 (1981/82)

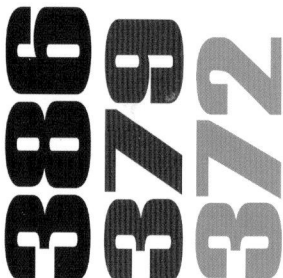

MOST GAMES PLAYED

Robert Parish: **1,611** (1976–1997)

Kareem Abdul-Jabbar: **1,560** (1969–1989)

MOST POINTS IN A SEASON

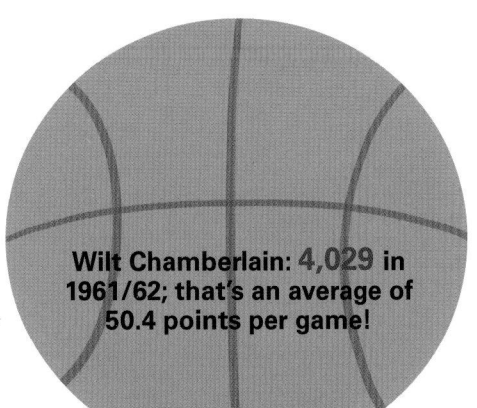

Wilt Chamberlain: 4,029 in 1961/62; that's an average of 50.4 points per game!

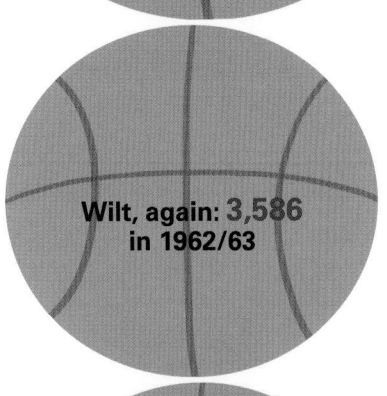

Wilt, again: 3,586 in 1962/63

Michael Jordan: 3,041 in 1986/87

A special nod goes to Elgin Baylor. He was on the LA Lakers roster in 1962, but he was also in the army. He was only allowed to play on weekends. But he was so good that he still scored nearly 1,836 points in just 48 games!

MOST REBOUNDS

Wilt Chamberlain: 23,924 (1960–1973)
Bill Russell: 21,620 (1966–1988)

HIGHEST CAREER POINTS AVERAGE (PER GAME)

Michael Jordan: 30.12 (1984–1993, 1995–1998, 2001–2003)
Wilt Chamberlain: 30.07 (1959–1973)
Kevin Durant: 27.40 (2007–present)

MOST CAREER POINTS

Kareem Abdul-Jabbar: 38,387 (1970–1989); that's an average of about 25 points per game.
Karl Malone: 36,928 (1985–2004)

YOUNGEST PLAYER TO REACH 1,000 POINTS

LeBron James was just 19 years and 41 days old when he reached 1,000 points.
He's also the youngest to reach 5,000, 10,000, 15,000, 20,000, and 25,000 points.

FOR THE RECORD BOOKS— TEAMS

Team records are also amazing but true!

LONGEST GAME

NBA: Indianapolis vs. Rochester, January 6, 1951—six overtimes (Indiana won, 75–73)

WNBA: Washington vs. Seattle, July 3, 2001—four overtimes (Washington won, 72–69)

MOST POINTS IN A GAME

NBA: Detroit scored 186 in a 1983 win over Denver

WNBA: Phoenix scored 127 in a 2010 win over Denver

FEWEST POINTS IN A GAME

NBA: Chicago scored 49 in a 1999 loss to Miami

WNBA: Washington scored 34 in a 2001 loss to Cleveland

MOST CHAMPIONSHIPS

Boston: 17
The Lakers: 16 (5 as the Minneapolis Lakers and 11 as the LA Lakers)

MOST APPEARANCES

The Lakers have appeared in the most finals—31—for a 51% winning percentage. Boston is next with 21 finals—an 81% winning percentage.

MOST WINS IN A SEASON

NBA: 73 by Golden State in 2015/16 (an 89% win percentage)
NBA: 72 by Chicago in 1995/96 (an 88% win percentage)
WNBA: 29 by Phoenix in 2014 (an 85% win percentage)

MOST LOSSES

NBA: 73 by Philadelphia in 1972/73
NBA: 72 by Philadelphia in 2015/16
WNBA: 31 by Tulsa in 2001

WINS IN A ROW

NBA: 33 by the Los Angeles Lakers in 1971/72

WNBA: 18 by LA in 2001

PLAY-OFF PANDEMONIUM!

The play-offs are the goal for every team that hits the hardwood. But when there are lots of teams and only a few spots, it can get tough.

NBA PLAY-OFF FORMAT

The NBA has 30 teams. Only 16 make the play-offs. That's a 53% shot. All rounds are best-of-seven.

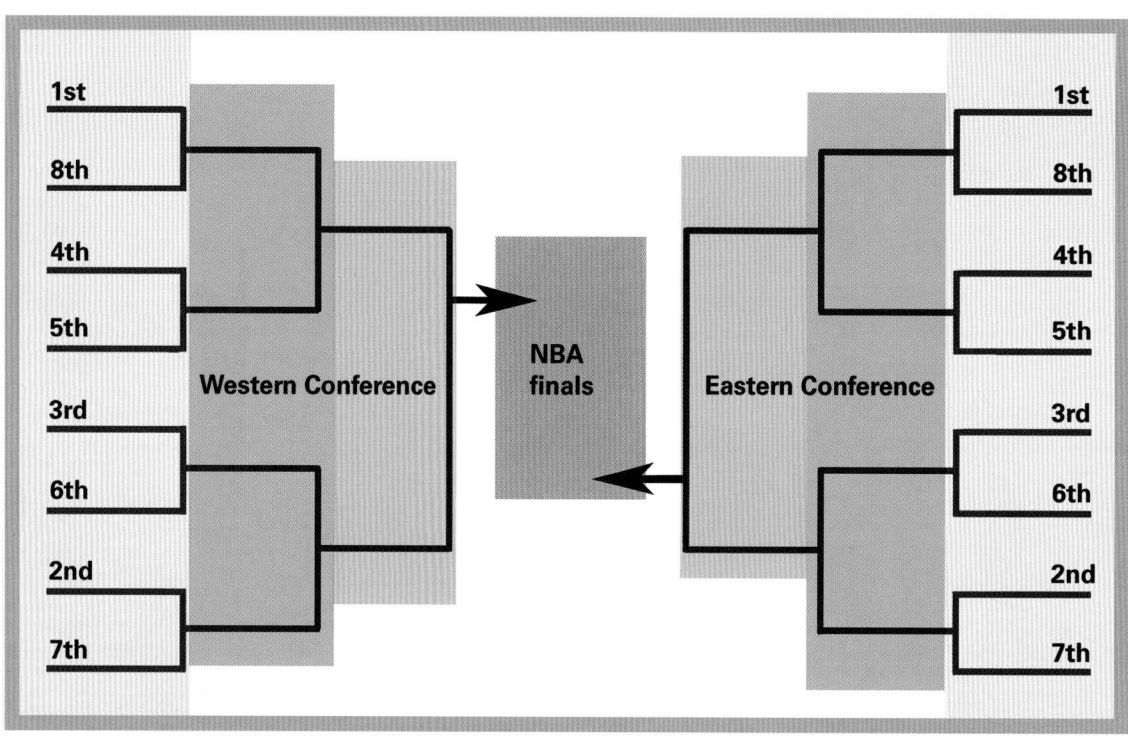

The top eight teams from each conference make the first round:

1 vs. 8
2 vs. 7
3 vs. 6
4 vs. 5

Eight teams advance to the conference semifinals (27%).

Four teams make the conference finals (13%).

Two make the final (6%).

The playoffs can take a looooooooong time. The 2016 *finals* took 7 games and 18 days to complete, with the championship game on June 19. The play-offs had STARTED on April 16—a total of 64 days. By contrast, the 1950 play-offs started March 21 and ended April 23—a total of 33 days.

WNBA PLAY-OFF FORMAT

The WNBA has 12 teams and their play-off format is VERY different.
The top eight WNBA teams make the play-offs.
Then they are seeded by record.

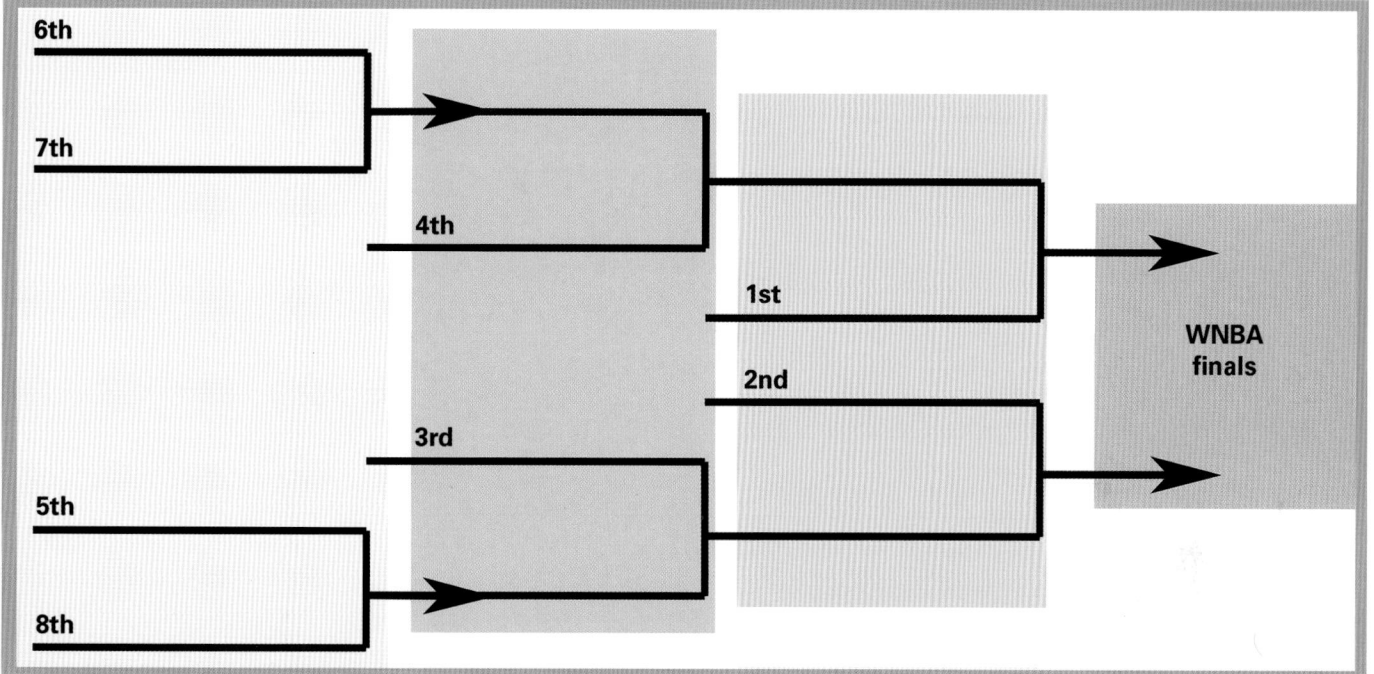

The lowest four teams meet in a one-game first round:
5 vs. 8
6 vs. 7
	Teams 3 and 4 wait for the second round.
	    The second round is also a one-game round:
	    3 vs. the lowest seed that won in the first round, and 4 vs. the other team that won in the first round.
	    The two teams that win in this round advance to the semis.

The teams that had the two best records in the regular season automatically go to the semifinals. This is a best-of-five series.

The winners of this round meet in the best-of-five finals.

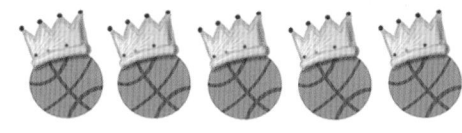

PLAY-OFF RECORDS

Most championships (by player):

Bill Russell (Boston Celtics)—**11**

Sam Jones (Boston Celtics)—**10**

Tom Heinsohn (Boston Celtics)—**8**

K.C. Jones (Boston Celtics)—**8**

Tom Sanders (Boston Celtics)—**8**

John Havlicek (Boston Celtics)—**8**

Jim Loscutoff (Boston Celtics)—**7**

Frank Ramsey (Boston Celtics)—**7**

Robert Horry (Houston, LA, and San Antonio)—**7**

OFFENSE VS. DEFENSE: THE NUMBERS

Sports and mathematics have become very close friends, and the stats generated for each player help tell you what's going on. Dwayne Dunker is on offense. Carrie Cager is trying to stop him. Stats can tell you a lot about how well each player does their job.

36.9 MIN:
Average minutes played. The higher the number, the more important the player is to the team. This player is a starter.

78
GP: Games played

1830
PTS: Points

23.5
PPG: Average points per game (1830 ÷ 78)

7.9
FGM: Field goals (baskets) made (614 ÷ 78)

17.7
FGA: Field goals attempted (1377 ÷ 78)

47
3PM: Three-point shots made total (0.6 per game average)

139
3PA: Three-point shots attempted (1.8 per game average)

44.6%
FG%:
Field goal percentage
A huge stat that
indicates Dwayne's
shooting accuracy
(614 FGM ÷ 1377
FGA)

555
FT:
Free throws
made
(7.1 per game
average)

64
OREB:
Offensive
rebounds
(0.8 per game
average)

85.4%
FT%:
Free throw
shooting
percentage
(555 FT ÷ 650
FTA)

650
FTA:
Free throws
attempted
(8.4 per game
average)

315
AST:
Assists
(4 per game
average)

46
STL:
Steals
(0.6 per game
average)

33.8%
3P%:
Three-point
shooting
percentage
(47 3PM ÷ 139
3PA)

17
BLK:
Blocked shots
(0.2 per game
average)

175
TOV:
Turnovers
(2.2 per game
average)

148
DREB:
Defensive
rebounds
(1.9 per game
average)

79
GP:
Games
played

167
PF:
Personal fouls
(2.1 per game
average) *

105
PF:
Personal fouls
(1.3 per game
average) *

14
GS:
Games started
(This player is
usually on the
bench.)

18.3
MIN:
Average minutes
played per player
per game

* If a player commits 6 fouls they
are kicked out of the game.

THE COLLEGE GAME

National College Athletic Association (NCAA) basketball is almost as popular as, if not more so than, the NBA and WNBA. Millions of fans watch the games, and thousands of athletes play.

There are NCAA basketball teams with long histories—both men's and women's—and surprising upstart teams as well.

Women formed the first college teams. Students from Smith College, a private women's college in Massachusetts, were playing the game in 1892. Later that year, the University of California, Berkeley, played an exhibition game against Miss Head's School from Oakland. The women's game was also being played in the Southern US—at Sophie Newcomb College (now part of Tulane University). They even played a public exhibition game in 1895. The first official intercollegiate women's game was played in 1896 between Stanford and Berkeley.

Vanderbilt had the first men's college team in 1893. They played a team from the YMCA. The first official men's college game was played in 1895, between teams from Hamline and Minnesota A&M.

FAIR PLAY?

Some people have called for college players to get paid. Right now, they get booted from their teams if they accept money to play or for endorsements. But players generate millions of dollars for their schools in ticket sales, TV rights, and merchandise.

Top salary for a college player? $0.

Top scholarship value for an NCAA player? Full tuition of about $30,000 year.

Top salary for a college coach? Mike Krzyzewski of Duke University gets paid $7 *million* dollars a year.

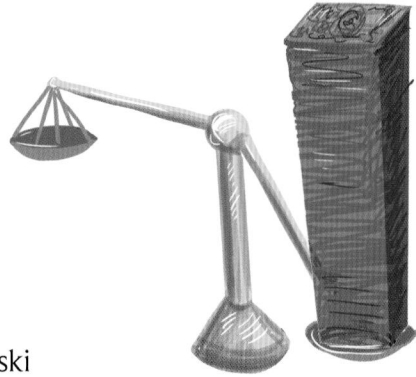

MARCH MADNESS

One of the biggest sporting events in the world is the NCAA March Madness tournament, when a small college from Washington can unseat a superpower from Kentucky.

The first national tournament was held in 1939. Eight teams were included.

In 1951, it grew to 16 and then, the year after that, to 22. And it's been growing ever since.

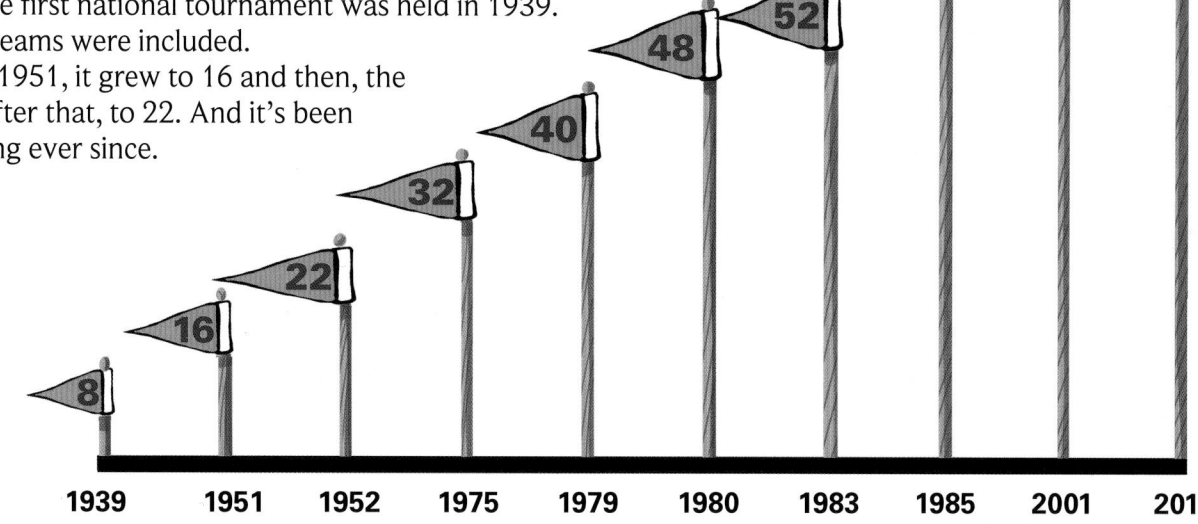

| 1939 | 1951 | 1952 | 1975 | 1979 | 1980 | 1983 | 1985 | 2001 | 2011 |

Since 2011, 68 teams have made each tournament, which covers much of March and April. There's a "First Four" round of games between eight of the teams—the formula is a bit complicated, but these games are usually between lower-ranked teams. The four winners of those games advance to the first round. The 64 teams that remain are ranked from 1 to 16 in four divisions, and then the madness begins.

It's a hard tournament to qualify for. Harvard made it in 1946, but didn't return till 2012, 66 years later.

Yale went 54 years—from 1962 to 2016—without playing. Tennessee Tech has the longest ongoing streak—they haven't qualified since 1963.

UCLA has won 11 titles. Kentucky is next with 8.

WOMEN'S MARCH MADNESS

The women's tournament was first held in 1982. There were 32 teams. Louisiana Tech beat Cheyney State, 76–62. Today, 64 teams make the women's tournament. Connecticut has won the most titles with 11. Tennessee has won 8 times.

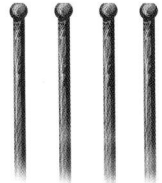
Four teams that are in the top divisions of the NCAA have never made it: Army, The Citadel, St. Francis Brooklyn, and William and Mary.

WHEELCHAIR WONDERS

Wheelchair sports became popular following World War II, when disabled veterans began to play games against one other. US veterans decided basketball would be perfect, and the sport grew quickly.

Many of the soldiers who fought in the war had been great athletes. But many of them also lost limbs in the fight.

That didn't stop their desire to play; it just changed the way they did it. A number of veterans found themselves at the Stoke Mandeville rehabilitation hospital in England. There, Dr. Ludwig Guttmann began using sports as part of the rehab, and, as often happens in sports, the games became more and more competitive. So in 1947, he organized a big sporting event—the Stoke Mandeville Games (they are still held). Wheelchair *netball* was featured. (It's similar to basketball, but with no backboards, dribbling, or running with the ball.)

Basketball was introduced a few years later. US veterans had begun forming basketball teams back home, and in 1956, a team called the Pan-Am Jets was invited to Stoke Mandeville. They won the first title easily and convinced organizers that basketball was actually better than netball. Wheelchair basketball grew globally, with teams in England, the Netherlands, France, and elsewhere signing on.

Netball

Basketball

Today, there are more than

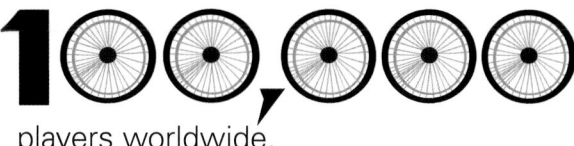

100,000

players worldwide.

The sport is part of the Paralympic Games and has its own world championships.

The first men's world championship was held in 1973 in Belgium. Great Britain won. The United States has won the most titles, with six.

The first women's world championship was held in 1990. The United States won. Canada has won more titles overall, with five.

COOL TEAM NAMES

Early teams were the Kansas City Bulldozers, California Flying Wheels, New Jersey Wheelers, and Vancouver Powerglides. The Montreal team was originally called The Paraplegics. When a sportswriter commented that he felt wonderment at watching them play, they renamed themselves the Wheelchair Wonders.

THE SCIENCE OF SPORT

Wheelchair basketball has some slightly different rules—and a truly cool chair.

The wheelchairs athletes use today are specially designed, with lower seats and wheels that are angled outward from the top. The lower center of gravity makes them more stable and prevents tipping (physics again!). They also have an extra set of castors (small wheels) at the front, also to help prevent tipping.

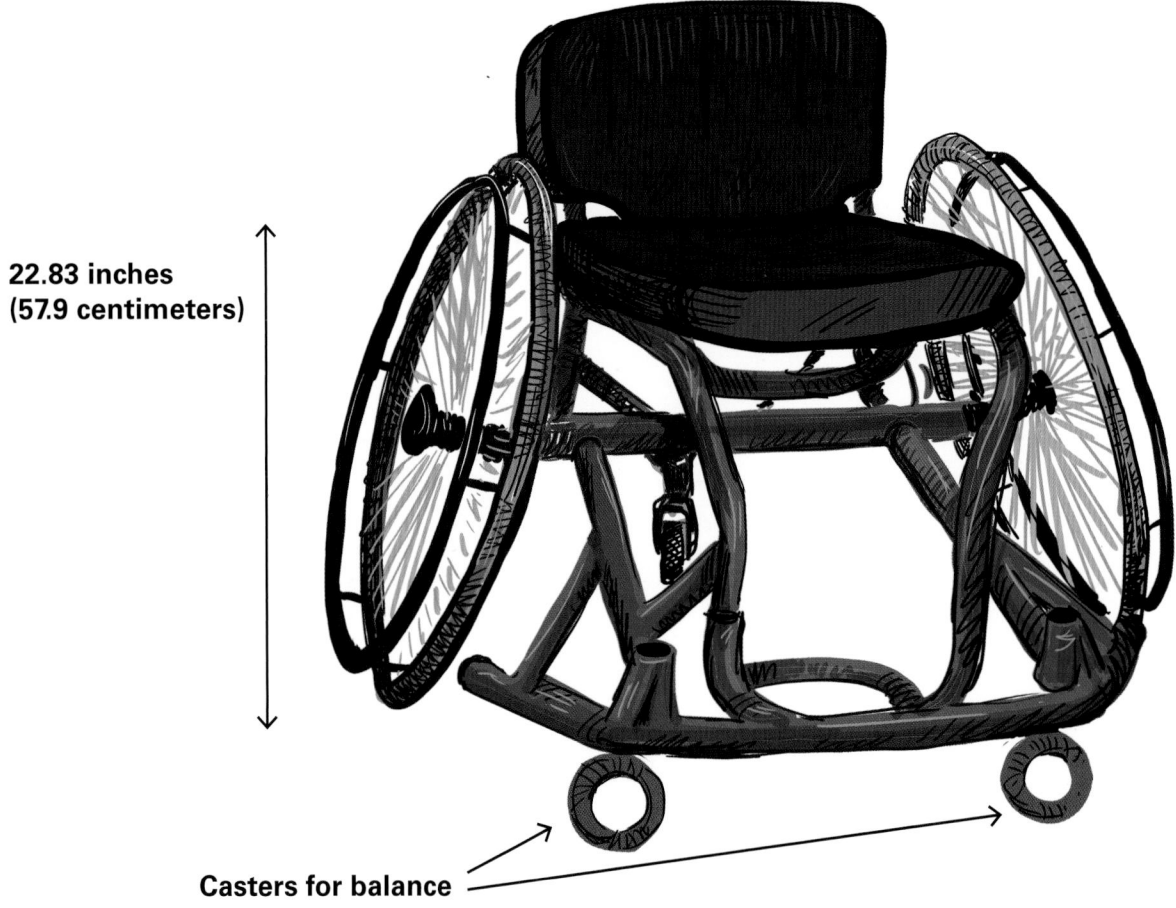

**22.83 inches
(57.9 centimeters)**

Casters for balance

27 inches (68.6 centimeters)

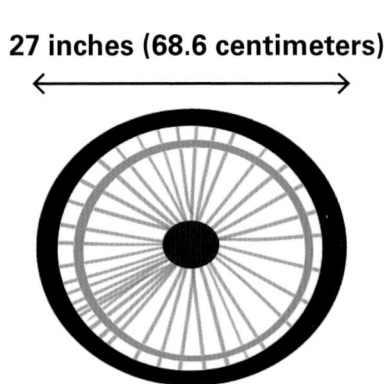

For players at the highest level, the chair height can't be more than 22.83 inches (57.9 centimeters) from the floor to the top of the seat. And the wheels can have a maximum diameter of 27 inches (68.6 centimeters).

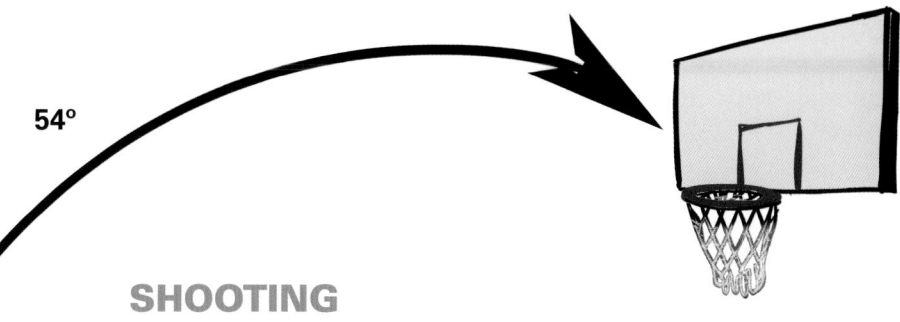

54°

SHOOTING

The angle of a shot is also different in a wheelchair because the shooter is closer to the surface of the court. Researchers at the University of Saskatchewan have calculated that for wheelchair basketball, an angle of 54 degrees is ideal. (You may remember that it was closer to 50 degrees for standing basketball.)

DRIBBLING

Wheelchair basketball rules are mostly the same as in the traditional game. The baskets are 10 feet (3.04 meters) high on a standard-sized court. Even the foul lines are the same.

But, the wheelchair is considered part of the player, so contact rules include contact with the chair. And dribbling is a big exception. Players can carry the ball (or rest it in their laps), but only for two pushes on their wheels. Then, they either have to dribble again, shoot, or pass.

1   **2**   **Bounce**   **Pass or shoot**

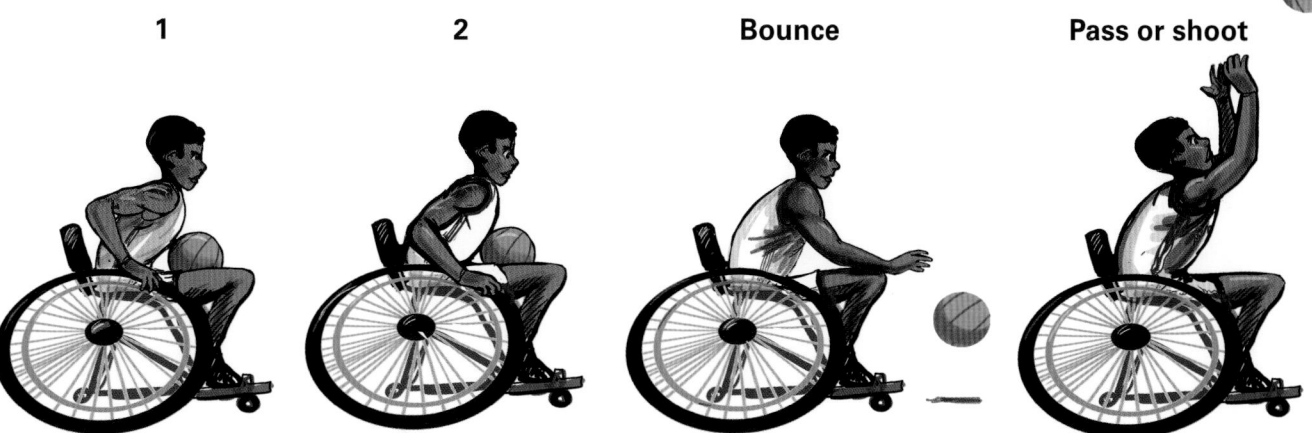

UNDERHANDED SHOTS

Cheating is as old as sports itself. So is bad behavior. Basketball has featured in some of the biggest scandals in sports.

1972 Olympics: The former Soviet Union (USSR) allegedly rigged the shot clock to give their team three chances to beat the United States in the men's final. (It kept "breaking" with three seconds left, giving the USSR chance after chance to shoot.) They won on a buzzer-beater (a shot that goes in right as the clock hits zero). The United States team was so mad, they refused their silver medals.

2000: The Spanish Paralympic basketball team was disqualified when it turned out many of the players were only *pretending* to qualify in the mentally challenged category.

2007: Basketball referee Tim Donaghy was accused of betting on games he was officiating. He was charged with helping teams score more points than expected. He pled guilty to numerous allegations and was sentenced to more than a year in prison.

1997: Player Latrell Sprewell was known for his temper. He and his Golden State coach P.J. Carlesimo would get into some epic yelling matches. During one practice, Sprewell got so angry that he choked Carlesimo, then later punched him. The NBA suspended Sprewell for 68 games.

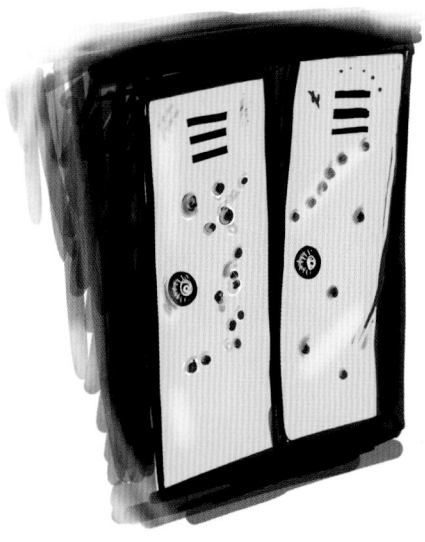

2009: Washington's Gilbert Arenas repeatedly got caught leaving guns in his locker. This was against NBA rules … and the law. One day, he and teammate Javaris Crittenton got into a fight over a $1,000 bet in a card game. Arenas grabbed a gun from his locker. Turned out Crittenton had one, too. A teammate talked them down, but the NBA suspended both players for the rest of the season.

FAILING GRADES

College basketball players have to keep up their grades if they want to stay on the team ... that's the rule, anyway. It isn't always followed.

Harvard's team was suspended from games in 1999 when it was discovered that some of its players were paying other students to do their homework. Seems they didn't learn their lesson: it happened again 12 years later!

But don't just blame Harvard.

Minnesota was stripped of its semifinal berth in 1997 after it turned out the team had hired a tutor to write papers for a number of players.

At Syracuse, one player didn't have high enough grades to stay on the team, but he was given a chance to redo and resubmit a paper. The second paper got a better grade. Yay! Except it turned out that the paper was written by the director of basketball operations and a basketball facility receptionist. Syracuse's head coach said that "breaking the rules" was different from cheating. What now? The NCAA banned the player for nine games.

At the University of North Carolina, more than a thousand basketball players over a span of 18 years took a "course" that never actually met, didn't require homework, and had just one required essay ... which got a high grade no matter what was on the paper.

A NIGHT OUT

It can cost a lot to go to a basketball game—a lot more than it used to cost your old aunt Nellie, that's for sure.

One reason things are more expensive today is inflation. Costs go up, and so a dollar buys less and less. So, it would take $8 of today's money to buy what $1 got you in 1960. But still, based on 1960 prices, a ticket should only cost about $10 today. The other factor in higher costs is "markup." This is how much extra you are charged for, say, a soda on top of what the concession stand paid for it.

1960

ticket: $1.50
courtside ticket: $4
(it wasn't such a big deal back then)

60¢

30¢

25¢

25¢

20¢

50¢

50¢

Let's say the concession stand buys the soda for about 50¢. It charges you $6.50. In other words, it makes a $6 profit from that soda. Now, that profit also goes to pay the salaries of the employees, the fees the concession stand might have to pay the arena to be there in the first place, and all sorts of other costs. But just compare what a soda might cost you at a store (about $2) and how much more you pay at a game.

No wonder most sporting venues don't let you bring in outside food!

Today

ticket: $40
courtside ticket: $2,000

souvenir cap: $25

program: $5

$7

$7

$7

$6

$9

$6.50

SOME ARENAS OFFER PRETTY UNUSUAL FOOD OPTIONS

Memphis sells Double-Fried Twinkies—$5 (and a whopping 900 calories!).
Orlando has blackened shrimp and avocado flatbread—$15.
Or there's the OMG hot dog (wrapped in pastrami) for $12.
New Orleans has a seafood mac 'n' cheese for $12.

MONEY IN, MONEY OUT

Basketball players get paid millions. Fans pay more and more for tickets. How does the pro-basketball economy work? Where does the money come from, and where does it go? Let's look at the estimated income and costs of running an average NBA team.

Money In
(ESTIMATED VALUES)

ticket sales:	$48,000,000
national TV revenue:	$9,000,000
local TV revenue:	$40,000,000
equipment partnerships (balls, shoes, uniforms):	$30,000,000
advertising sales and sponsorship deals:	$23,000,000
international sales of TV rights, merchandise:	$11,000,000
food sales:	$10,000,000
play-off revenue:	$6,000,000
Total in:	**$177,000,000**

Money Out

(ESTIMATED VALUES)

player salaries:	$87,000,000
employee salaries and office costs:	$26,000,000
arena costs (rent and operations):	$5,000,000
scouting and player development:	$4,000,000
advertising:	$5,000,000
insurance on players:	$3,480,000
local taxes:	$5,000,000
interest and payments on debt:	$6,000,000
long-term debt:	$117,000,000*
Total out:	**$141,480,000**

Total in: **$177,000,000**

Total out: **–$141,480,000**

Net profit: **$35,520,000**

*DEBT LOADS

Some of the profit goes to pay down the team's total debt, and that amount can change from year to year. But why does a basketball team have debt? Some of it could come from buying the team from a previous owner (Steve Ballmer bought the LA Clippers in 2014 for $2 billion), and some might be leftover from the costs of buying or building a new arena.

Not all teams have debt. But not all profit stays as profit, either. Some goes to pay federal taxes, injury insurance payouts, and other unexpected costs. What's left might be reinvested or paid out to people who own stock in the team.

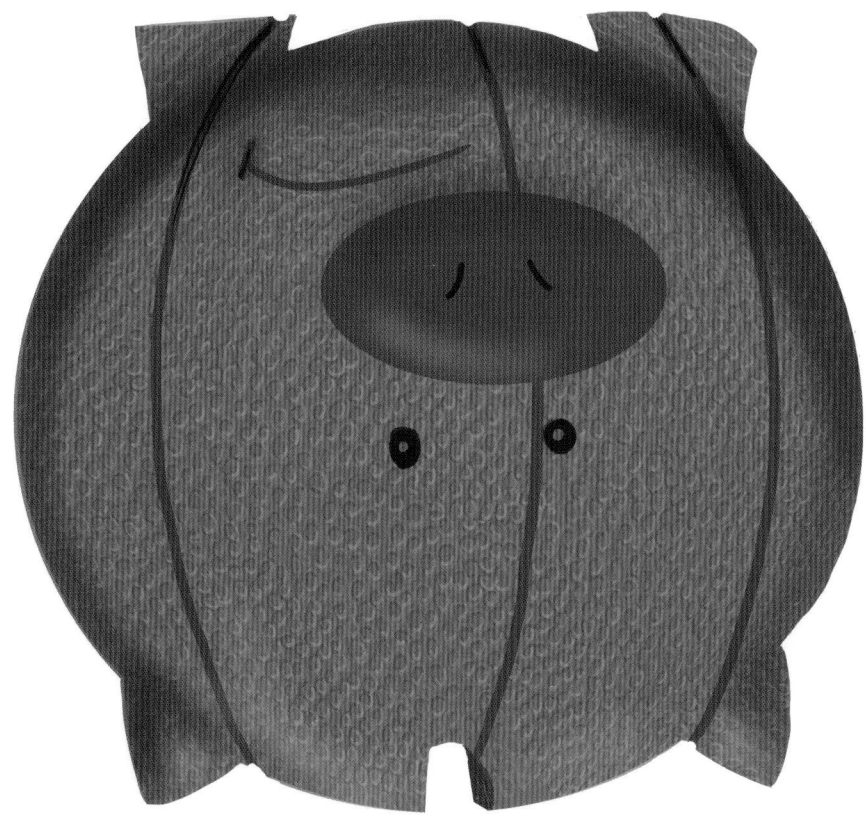

WHO'S WATCHING?

The NBA has seen some rough times; but recently, TV ratings and attendance have been skyrocketing.

The NBA has been in tons of financial trouble in the past. It just wasn't that popular. In the 1970s, *championship* games were shown tape-delayed on late-night TV. But things started to turn around in the 1980s, and now, the sky's the limit.

TOTAL NBA ATTENDANCE (AND AVERAGE PER GAME)

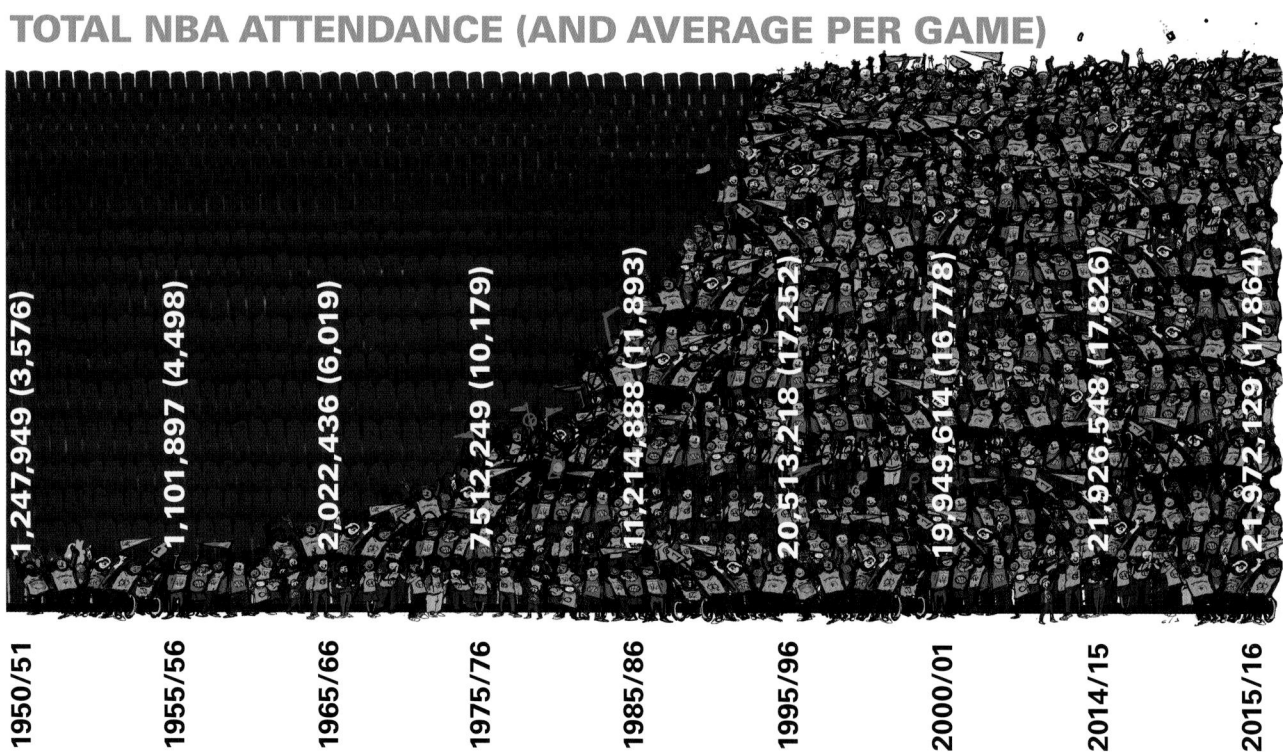

Year	Total (Average)
1950/51	1,247,949 (3,576)
1955/56	1,101,897 (4,498)
1965/66	2,022,436 (6,019)
1975/76	7,512,249 (10,179)
1985/86	11,214,888 (11,893)
1995/96	20,513,218 (17,252)
2000/01	19,949,614 (16,778)
2014/15	21,926,548 (17,826)
2015/16	21,972,129 (17,864)

AVERAGE NUMBER OF WNBA FANS PER GAME

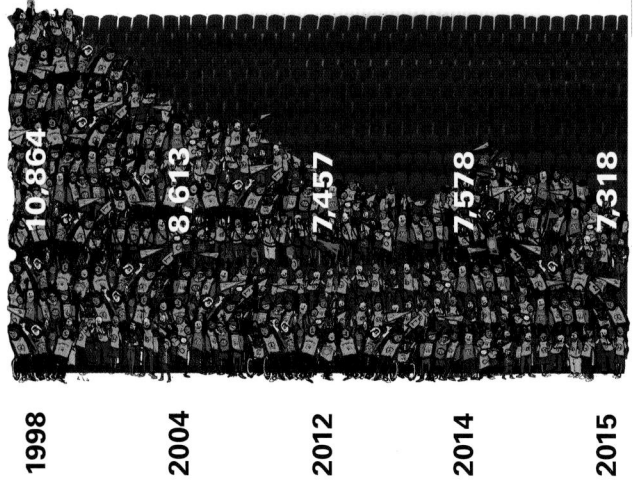

Year	Average
1998	10,864
2004	8,613
2012	7,457
2014	7,578
2015	7,318

WNBA ATTENDANCE HAS ACTUALLY DIPPED IN RECENT YEARS.

TV RATINGS

The NBA Finals are a good test of the popularity of the league. Here's an average number of viewers per game according to the US ratings (since they started being shown live):

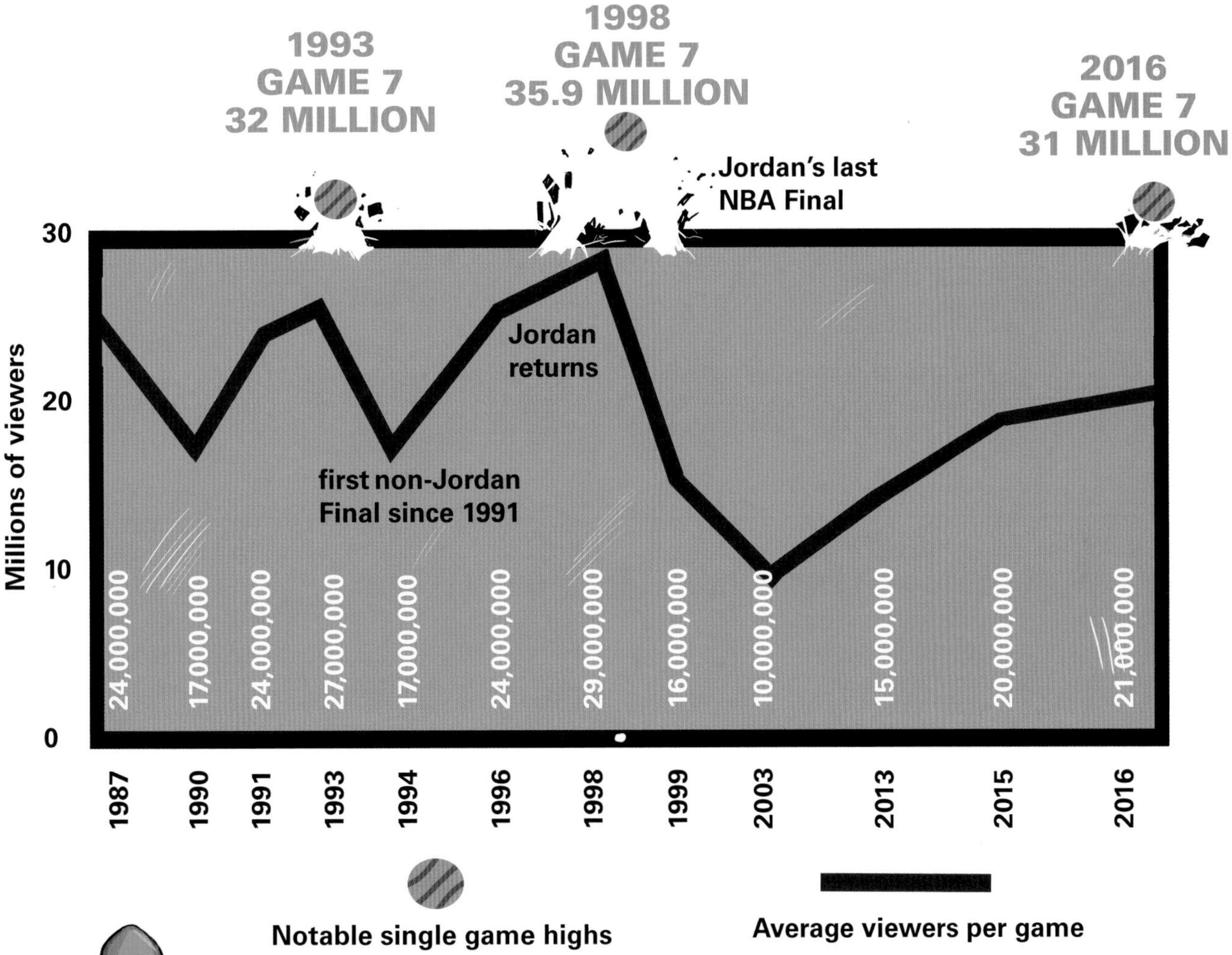

1993
GAME 7
32 MILLION

1998
GAME 7
35.9 MILLION

2016
GAME 7
31 MILLION

Jordan's last
NBA Final

Jordan
returns

first non-Jordan
Final since 1991

Millions of viewers

24,000,000	17,000,000	24,000,000	27,000,000	17,000,000	24,000,000	29,000,000	16,000,000	10,000,000	15,000,000	20,000,000	21,000,000
1987	1990	1991	1993	1994	1996	1998	1999	2003	2013	2015	2016

 **Notable single game highs**

Average viewers per game

MICHAEL JORDAN

It's hard to overstate the importance of Michael Jordan to the NBA. He hasn't played for the Chicago Bulls for two decades, but the team still sells the most merchandise globally. He made six NBA Finals and won all six. In 1993, he averaged 41 points a game, still an NBA record. He's the modern standard for excellence in the game.

GLOBAL GROWTH

NBA ratings are going to grow. Already, more than 200 countries broadcast the NBA Finals, in 50 different languages. The NBA estimates that more than 250 million people follow the games—by watching, streaming, or through social media.

The NBA recently signed a deal with Chinese Internet company Tencent to show live games and other programming. Tencent is paying the NBA $100 million a year for five years for the rights.

A DIFFERENT KIND OF CAP

Owners and players often fight over the best way to divvy up profits, sales, and income. The NBA was one of the first leagues to introduce a salary cap. But it changes every year, and there are some truly weird loopholes.

The NBA adopted a salary cap in 1984.

Before that, teams could bid for the top players. The problem, from the league's perspective, was that the rich teams could buy all the best players, shutting out the poor teams. Poor teams were then stuck with weak players that no one wanted to see ... and those teams were always in danger of folding or moving.

So, the league set a limit—or "cap"—on what a team could spend on player salaries per year: a total of $3.6 million (or about $8 million in today's dollars).

That year, Magic Johnson earned more than $2 million with the LA Lakers—or more than half of the team's total available salary dollars. That meant the team had to pay 90% of its players with less than 50% of its salary dollars. A tough balancing act.

The cap is linked to how much money the league makes. The average cap is about 50% of total revenues. So the owners get half and all the players get half.

The good news for everyone is that revenues have risen pretty steadily since 1984. So the cap jumped from $3.6 million in that first year to $4.2 million in 1985, then rose to about $10 million in 1990 and $20 million in 1995. And it keeps growing:

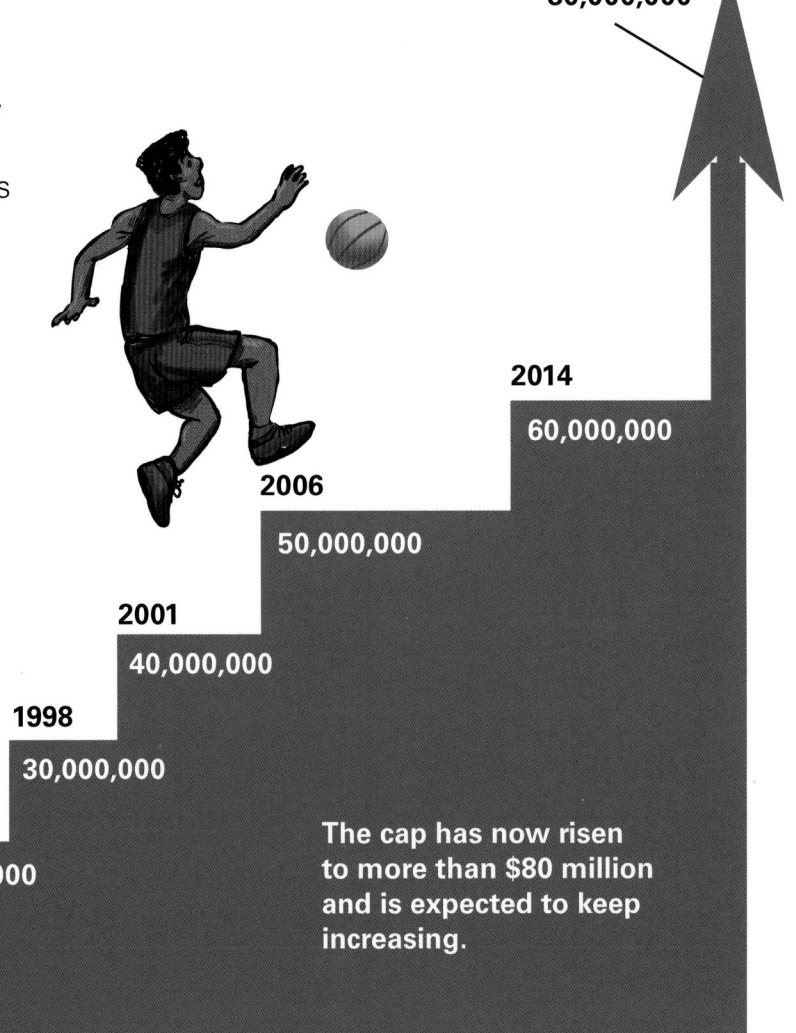

Today
80,000,000

2014
60,000,000

2006
50,000,000

2001
40,000,000

1998
30,000,000

1995
20,000,000

1984
3,600,000

1990
10,000,000

1985
4,200,000

The cap has now risen to more than $80 million and is expected to keep increasing.

BUT WAIT ...

The NBA's cap is what's known as a "soft cap." That means teams can actually pay more than the salary cap, but they get penalized for it.

But they don't necessarily get penalized ... Are you following along?

There are some players teams can designate as "special" (superstars, basically), and teams can pay them more than the cap limit would normally allow. But they have to be careful.

PENALTIES

If they go way OVER the cap, they have to pay a penalty that gets split up amongst the poorer teams.

The more they spend over the cap, the higher the penalty.

The Brooklyn Nets got dinged in 2013/14. They had a lot of old contracts to honor and they also signed a bunch of new players to big contracts.

That put them so far over the cap that they paid more than $90 million in penalties alone. But the team had just relocated from New Jersey and became competitive very quickly, so maybe the price tag was worth it for the owner and fans.

Teams can spend under the cap or at the cap with no penalty.

The salary cap is set by the contract between the owners and the league—the collective bargaining agreement, or CBA. It can be long and complicated.

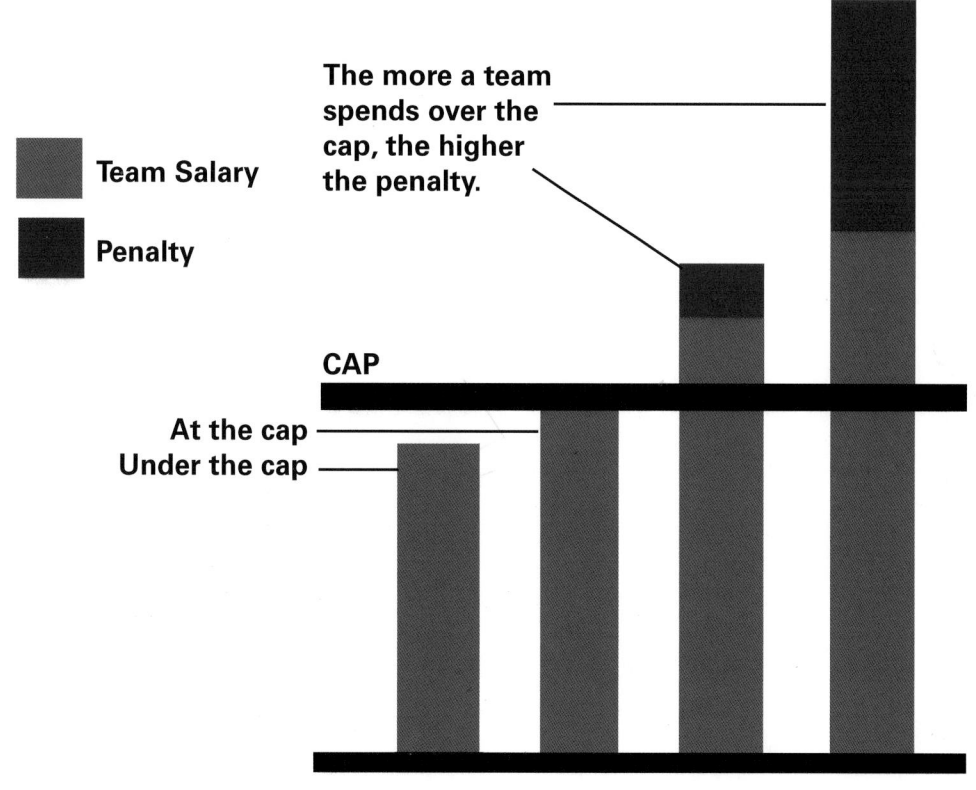

Team Salary

Penalty

The more a team spends over the cap, the higher the penalty.

CAP

At the cap

Under the cap

DIFFERENT AT THE TOP

The NBA is global and multicultural … on the court. The further you get from the court, though, the less multicultural it gets.

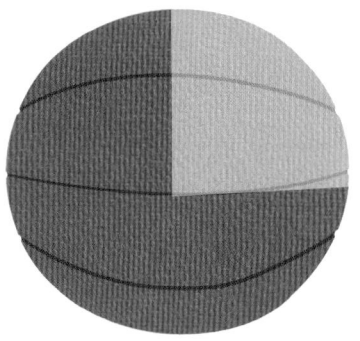

About 75% of NBA players are African-American.

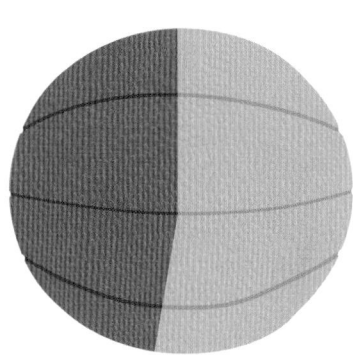

About 55% of coaches are white (compared to about 10% in the NFL and MLB).

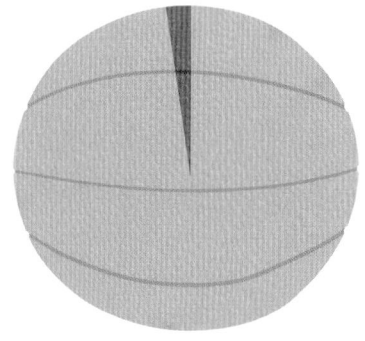

Ownership is *very* white. A few exceptions: Former NBA superstar Michael Jordan owns the Charlotte Hornets. Vivek Ranadivé—who's originally from India—owns Golden State. It's also very male. Two owners are women—Gail Miller (Utah) and Jeanie Buss (LA Lakers). Both inherited the teams from their husbands. The other 26 teams are owned by white men.

 African-American

White

Hispanic

WNBA

The situation isn't much different in the **WNBA**. Atlanta is owned by Mary Brock and Kelly Loeffler. Seattle is co-owned by Dawn Trudeau, Lisa Brummel, and Ginny Gilder. The other 10 teams? You guessed it: owned by men!

AFRICAN-AMERICAN FANS

NFL
Only 13% of NFL fans identify as African-American.

NHL
Only 3% of NHL fans identify as African-American.

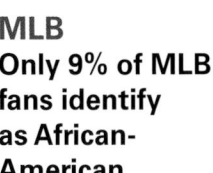
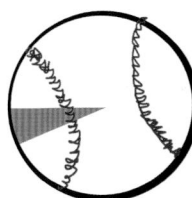

MLB
Only 9% of MLB fans identify as African-American.

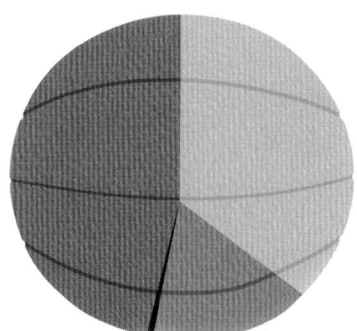

NBA audiences, on the other hand, are the most diverse of all the major sports.
45% are African-American
40% are white
12% are Hispanic
3% are other

MALE AND FEMALE FANS
NBA
70% of fans are men; 30% are women
NFL
65% of fans are men; 35% are women
MLB
70% of fans are men; 30% are women
NHL
68% of fans are men; 32% are women

COMING OUT
Jason Collins played 12 years in the **NBA**, and came out as gay for the last two of those. At the time, he was the only openly gay player in a major men's sports league. He retired in 2014. Numerous **WNBA** players identify as gay, including Sheryl Swoopes, Sharnee Zoll-Norman, and Brittney Griner.

THE ORIGINAL 13 RULES

The rules of basketball are simple. Here are the original 13 rules James Naismith wrote down for his game in 1891.

Basket Ball

1. The ball may be thrown in any direction with one or both hands.

2. The ball may be batted in any direction with one or both hands (never with the fist).

3. A player cannot run with the ball. The player must throw it from the spot on which he catches it, allowance to be made for a man who catches the ball when running at a good speed if he tries to stop.

4. The ball must be held in or between the hands; the arms or body must not be used for holding it.

5. No shouldering, holding, pushing, tripping, or striking in any way the person of an opponent shall be allowed; the first infringement of this rule by any player shall count as a foul, the second shall disqualify him till the next goal is made, or, if there was evident intent to injure the person, for the whole of the game, no substitute allowed.

6. A foul is striking at the ball with the fist, violation of Rules 3, 4, and such as described in Rule 5.

7. If either side makes three consecutive fouls, it shall count as a goal for the opponents (consecutive means without the opponents in the mean time making a foul).

8. A goal shall be made when the ball is thrown or batted from the ground into the basket and stays there, providing those defending the goal do not touch or disturb the goal. If the ball rests on the edges, and the opponent moves the basket, it shall count as a goal.

9. When the ball goes out of bounds, it shall be thrown into the field of play by the person first touching it. In case of a dispute, the umpire shall throw it straight into the field. The thrower-in is allowed five seconds; if he holds it longer, it shall go to the opponent. If any side persists in delaying the game, the umpire shall call a foul on that side.

10. The umpire shall be judge of the men and shall note the fouls and notify the referee when three consecutive fouls have been made. He shall have power to disqualify men according to Rule 5.

11. The referee shall be judge of the ball and shall decide when the ball is in play, in bounds, to which side it belongs, and shall keep the time. He shall decide when a goal has been made, and keep account of the goals with any other duties that are usually performed by a referee.

12. The time shall be two 15-minute halves, with 5 minutes' rest between.

13. The side making the most goals in that time shall be declared the winner. In case of a draw, the game may, by agreement of the captains, be continued till another goal is made.

Dec 1891 James Naismith

TRIVIA TIME

1. The Harlem Globetrotters were one of the first all-African-American professional teams, and are still one of the most popular traveling teams in the world. Where are they from?
a. Chicago
b. Baltimore
c. Harlem
d. Memphis

2. Match the team nickname to its ORIGINAL home.
Grizzlies (currently Memphis)   Minneapolis
Jazz (currently Utah)   Vancouver
Lakers (currently LA)   New Orleans

3. Jo Jackrabbit scores 35 points in his team win. Seven of those points came from free throws. Which of these statements can't be true?
a. Jo also made 10 baskets.
b. Jo also made 14 baskets.
c. Jo also made 15 baskets.
d. Jo made nine 3-point shots.

4. Women have been playing basketball almost as long as men. When was the first women's Olympic tournament held?
a. 1936
b. 1956
c. 1976
d. 1996

5. Michael Jordan was perhaps the greatest player of all time. But he took a year off from the NBA in 1993/94. What did he do instead?
a. He worked as a broadcaster.
b. He played baseball.
c. He sailed around the world.
d. He was sick.

6. Who was the first African-American player drafted by an NBA team?
a. Elgin Baylor
b. Earl Lloyd
c. Nat "Sweetwater" Clifton
d. Chuck Cooper

7. Canadian James Naismith wrote the original 13 rules for basketball. Where was the first game played?
a. Springfield, Massachusetts
b. Springfield, Illinois
c. Springfield, Connecticut
d. Springfield, Ontario

8. The WNBA was formed in 1996. Who won the first WNBA title?
a. Boston
b. San Antonio
c. Seattle
d. Houston

9. What team has won the most NBA titles?
a. Los Angeles
b. Golden State
c. Boston
d. New York

10. What is the name of the NBA championship trophy?
a. The Larry O'Brien Trophy
b. The Walter A. Brown Trophy
c. The Red Auerbach Trophy
d. It doesn't have a name.

11. What is the name of the WNBA championship trophy?
a. The Senda Berenson Trophy
b. The Laurel J. Ritchie Trophy
c. The Sheryl Swoopes Trophy
d. It doesn't have a name.

12. The NBA logo shows a player dribbling with the ball. Who is the design based on?
a. Wilt Chamberlain
b. Michael Jordan
c. Chuck Taylor
d. Jerry West

13. Why are basketball players called "cagers"?
a. The netting looks like a cage.
b. They played inside cage-like fences.
c. They play like fierce caged animals.

14. Which of these is not a nickname for a missed shot?
a. A brick
b. An airball
c. A layup
d. None of the above

15. Shaquille O'Neal is one of the greatest NBA players of all time. Opposing teams tried a tactic called Hack-a-Shaq. What was it?

16. Title IX revolutionized sport by making it illegal to discriminate against women. Before Title IX, there were about 30,000 women playing college sports. Today, it's more like 200,000. That's a rise of?
a. About 400%
b. About 500%
c. About 600%
d. About 700%

17. Basketball courts are made up of wood slats. Most are maple. Boston is an exception. What wood is the Celtics' floor made of?

THE ANSWERS

1. a) Chicago! The team's owner thought Harlem had more "mystique." The team didn't actually play a game in Harlem till 1968. Check our their website: www.harlemglobetrotters.com.

2. VANCOUVER Grizzlies
NEW ORLEANS Jazz
MINNEAPOLIS Lakers
www.nba.com has all the history you could want.

3. c) Joe scored 28 points on shots. But 15 baskets equals 30 points. Mathematically, it's not possible. But here's the cool thing about basketball: because you can score one-, two-, or three-point shots, almost any score between 1 and 2,000,001 is possible.

4. c) 1976
For more on women's basketball, check out www.wnba.com. There's also the Women's Basketball Hall of Fame in Knoxville, Tennessee. Its website is www.wbhof.com.

5. b) He tried out for the Chicago White Sox minor league baseball team. Jordan played for minor league teams in Birmingham and Scottsdale. He returned to the NBA in 1995. But his team, Chicago, had already retired his number! So, instead of #23, he wore #45.

6. d) Chuck Cooper. He was drafted by Boston in 1950. Lloyd was the first to play in an actual game. For more on the history of pre-integration basketball, check out the Black Fives Foundation at www.blackfives.org.

7. a) Springfield, Massachusetts. It's the home of the Naismith Hall of Fame (www.hoophall.com).

8. d) Houston. The Comets won the first four titles!

9. c) Boston. The Celtics have 17. The Lakers have 16 (5 in Minneapolis and 11 in LA). The Lakers have appeared in more finals—31—for a 51% winning percentage. Boston is next with 21 appearances—an 81% winning percentage.

10. a) The Larry O'Brien Trophy. It's named after former NBA Commissioner Larry O'Brien. (Fun fact: O'Brien was also once in charge of the US post office!) The trophy was called the Walter A. Brown Trophy up till 1984. Brown was the original owner of the Boston Celtics.

11. d) It doesn't have a name. The WNBA just refers to it as the Championship Trophy.

12. d) Jerry West. The designer of the logo says he loved the way the LA Laker Hall of Famer moved with the ball. (The NBA doesn't admit that it's a particular player.) The WNBA logo shows a woman shooting the ball, but they also say it's not based on any player.

13. b) They played inside cage-like fences. Often made of chicken wire, these fences kept players separated from the crowds in many early games.

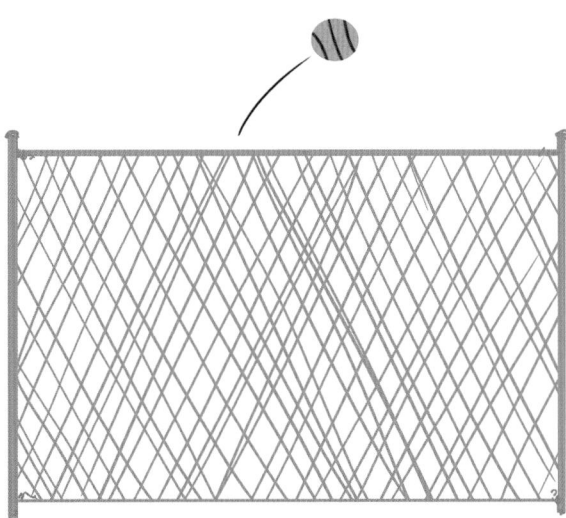

14. c) A layup. A layup is a shot that is bounced toward the hoop off the backboard.

15. Shaq was notoriously bad at free throws. So other teams (Dallas started it) would foul him all the time on purpose. The idea was that they'd rather give him easy shots that he missed than have him score more baskets.

16. c) About

600%

17. Oak. It's also a unique "parquet" pattern. Brooklyn has only been in the NBA a few years, but they also have a unique design known as a "herringbone" pattern. *Sports Illustrated* ran a neat story ranking all the NBA floor designs (www.si.com/nba/photo/2016/02/03/power-ranking-all-30-nba-floor-designs).

REFERENCES AND FURTHER READING

Did reading *Basketballogy* make you hungry for more? Great! There are many great resources out there to search, read, and get lost in. Here are specific sources for some of the stories inside the book.

Pages 6 and 7: The James Naismith quote is taken from a radio interview Naismith gave in 1936. You can hear the interview on the website for Kansas University. (Naismith began coaching there in 1898.)
www.exhibits.lib.ku.edu/exhibits/show/naismith150

Pages 12 and 13: The City College of New York has a bunch of amazing stuff on their digital archives, including a timeline of the evolution of pro basketball. There are lots of cool tidbits, including the info about Yale University's men's team being the first to use dribbling in a game.
digital-archives.ccny.cuny.edu/exhibits/holman/timeline.html

And, of course, you can also check out *www.nba.com* for info on the NBA.

Page 17: The WNBA has a great website with information on rules, schedules, and great players.
www.wnba.com

Page 21: Yes, it can be unnerving to take a foul shot at Arizona State. *The New York Times* reported on the effect in 2015.
www.nytimes.com/2015/02/14/upshot/how-arizona-state-reinvented-free-throw-distraction.html

Page 25: The researchers at North Carolina State University published their research in the *Journal of Quantitative Analysis in Sports*: Vol. 7: Issue 1, Article 3.

But there's a great breakdown of the study on the website for *Wired* magazine.
https://www.wired.com/2011/03/physics-basketball-shots/

Pages 28 and 29: Information about the value for Air Jordan shoes is taken from
www.espn.com/nba/story/_/id/12465427/michael-jordan-nba-shoes-1984-go-auction.

Pages 30 and 31: The Magic Shoe/Age trick is explained in a number of places. This one for example:
www.realclearscience.com/blog/2014/10/the_math_behind_the_shoe_size-age_trick_108920.html

Pages 32 and 33: There is a great website on the history of African-American basketball.
www.blackfives.org

Pages 34 and 35: We worked out the racial makeup of NBA rosters in 1950 by going through the information on *www.basketball-reference.com.*

You could lose yourself for days looking up amazing information on that site!

Pages 36 and 37: Senda Berenson was truly amazing. You can find a good bio for her on *https://jwa.org.*

Pages 38 and 39: Sheryl Swoopes has her own website, with lots of interesting photos and stories about her days as a pro player. *www.sherylswoopes.net*

Pages 42 and 43: The stats on how many people play various sports is taken from the stats as reported by the individual international sporting bodies.
www.fifa.com for soccer
www.fiba.com for basketball
www.iihf.com for hockey
www.ifaf.org for (American) football
www.itftennis.com for tennis
www.wbsc.org for baseball

Pages 50 and 51: You can search Youtube for lots of videos of amazing dunks. Search for "12-foot basket exhibition events" if you'd like to see some amazingly high dunks.

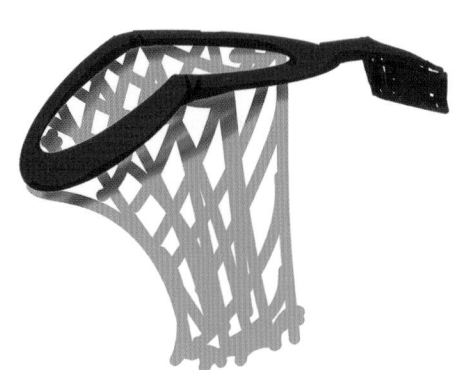

Pages 64 and 65: Information about Smith College's women's team is taken from the website for the Women's Basketball Hall of Fame.
www.wbhof.com
    You can visit the Hall in Knoxville, Tennessee. It features, among many amazing things, the world's largest basketball. It weighs 10 tons!

The NCAA website has lots of info, including stats for your chances of making it to the pros … and not just for basketball.
www.ncaa.org/about/resources/research/ probability-competing-beyond-high-school

If you'd like to read a little more about the first women's college game, check out this blog post:
www.californiagoldenblogs.com/ 2011/3/2/2005186/the-worlds- irst-womens-college-basketball- team-the-california-golden

Pages 74 and 75: It's hard to know exactly how much money NBA teams make or spend. But you can find some information out there. We checked out a lot of sources including *Forbes* magazine.
www.forbes.com/teams/toronto-raptors/
www.investopedia.com/articles/ investing/070715/nbas-business-model.asp
    And the website Deadspin does lots of great sports reporting. They took a look at the numbers they could find in this story.
www.deadspin.com/5816870/exclusive-how- and-why-an-nba-team-makes-a-7-million-profit- look-like-a-28-million-loss

Pages 76 and 77: Attendance figures are taken from the Association for Basketball Research.
www.apbr.org

INDEX

ABOUT KEVIN SYLVESTER

Kevin Sylvester grew up like lots of kids, with a basketball hoop in his backyard and a neighborhood full of basketball-loving kids.

He's a pretty good outside shooter, but at 5 feet 6 inches, he can only dream of actually dunking a ball. And yes, he does dream about that—a lot.

He used to watch the Niagara University Purple Eagles play, the men and the women, and still has a Purple Eagles patch his dad gave him. Dad (six feet tall) was a very good basketball player and taught philosophy at NU.

Kevin was a sportscaster with CBC Radio for many years and covered the Toronto Raptors and Vancouver Grizzlies in their early years.

It's hard to find a sport Kevin doesn't like. His book *Baseballogy* explored the great stories and stats behind baseball. *Game Day* introduced the people who work behind the scenes to put on sporting events. Both books were nominated for the Silver Birch Award.

The author in 1986, on his intramural college basketball team